MW01281942

It All Felt Impossible

ADVANCE PRAISE

"In *It All Felt Impossible: 42 Years in 42 Essays*, Tom McAllister taps into the collective worries and joys of us all by using experiences that while uniquely his own are ours, too. This reflective collection unfurls a life full of beauty, humor, curiosity, and wonder. It allows us to see that while the years may continue to roll on, our hearts and minds keep track of it all by anchoring us to what was and what can be."
—**Athena Dixon, author of *The Loneliness Files***

"People used to say, and maybe still do, that just before you die, your whole life flashes before your eyes. Leaving aside that if that were true, we the living wouldn't know it, *It All Felt Impossible* is a life flashing by in the form of a book, incredibly fast and unbelievably rich, in all its universal specificity—the good dogs and bad haircuts, first crushes and brushes with death, the memories we dream up (the fiction we all write), all the fear, grief, stupidity, hope, and joy we get to live through, as "a person who is alive." This book is so funny and honest, and so full of heart-breaking love."
—**Elisa Gabbert, author of *Any Person Is the Only Self***

"Tom McAllister's *It All Felt Impossible* is a beautiful portrait of a slow and tender passage of time, and what it is to live through several eras of a life with a sense of gratitude, humor, warmth, and generosity. I felt carried, warmly, through these many eras."
—**Hanif Abdurraqib, author of *There's Always This Year: On Basketball and Ascension***

"These are my favorite kinds of essays: honest, concise, funny, self-aware, and engaged with the world. Whether Tom McAllister is writing about dogs, jobs, marriage, death, friendship, sports, or anything else, *It All Felt Impossible* combines the brisk pace of a good memoir with the inquiry, insight, and breadth of the best essay collections. The result is one of the freshest and most engaging books I've read in years."
—**Justin St. Germain, author of *Son of a Gun: A Memoir***

42 Years in 42 Essays

It
All
Felt
Impossible

Tom McAllister

Rose Metal Press

2025

Copyright © 2025 by Tom McAllister

All rights reserved. No part of this book may be used or reproduced in any manner without written permission except in the case of brief quotations within critical articles and reviews. Please direct inquiries to:

Rose Metal Press, Inc.
P.O. Box 1956, Brookline, MA 02446
rosemetalpress@gmail.com
www.rosemetalpress.com

Library of Congress Cataloging-in-Publication Data

Names: McAllister, Tom, author.
Title: It all felt impossible : 42 years in 42 essays / by Tom McAllister.
Description: Brookline : Rose Metal Press, 2025.
Identifiers: LCCN 2024058471 (print) | LCCN 2024058472 (ebook) | ISBN
   9781941628355 (paperback) | ISBN 9781941628362 (ebook)
Subjects: LCSH: McAllister, Tom. | Authors, American--21st
   century--Biography. | LCGFT: Autobiographies. | Essays.
Classification: LCC PS3613.C2653 Z46 2025 (print) | LCC PS3613.C2653
   (ebook) | DDC 813/.6 [B]--dc23/eng/20241206
LC record available at https://lccn.loc.gov/2024058471
LC ebook record available at https://lccn.loc.gov/2024058472

Cover artwork by Cory Neale. More information and artwork at coryneale.com.

Cover and interior design by Heather Butterfield.

This book is manufactured in the United States of America and printed on acid-free paper.

CONTENTS

AUTHOR'S NOTE

Due to some quirks in publication schedules that are too boring to detail here, I found myself several years ago in the position of having two novels published within 13 months, by different presses, each with their own publicity cycles and ramp-ups and anxieties and minor successes and disappointments. One thing you have to do when you publish a book, besides all the edits and copyedits, is produce an extra 15,000 words or so of promotional text—email interviews and think pieces and craft essays and other little chunks of content that serve primarily to signal to the reading world that you are a person who exists, and your book is something that also exists.

I'm generally a fast writer, but this style of writing doesn't come naturally to me; during that 13-month period I felt like I was constantly churning out new words, not because I cared about them or believed in them but because I had to if I wanted anyone to buy my books, which were filled with words I *did* care about and believe in. I knew I was lucky to have one book out, let alone two, and I also understood I owed it to everyone involved in their publication to do the best work I could on these chunks of content, to reply enthusiastically when a publicist pitched me on an idea for a new 1,000-word chunk of content that I might be able to produce by next week, but ideally sooner if possible. To reply, "Thanks for thinking of me!" and then gnash my teeth about how terrifically persecuted I was to have to do homework on someone else's schedule. It was around this time that I became a habitual user of exclamation points in my emails, each one a forced smile. I never missed a deadline; I never felt there was more than minimal value in any of these individual chunks of content.

It would be inaccurate to say I was burned out; that's a word for people with harder lives and more important jobs than mine. But I was tired. As soon as I finished producing what I believed were the last of these chunks of content, I stopped writing completely for the rest of the year. This was a conscious choice at first, an attempt to recharge and find new things to say. Soon enough it became a condition I couldn't shake. I added items like "start a new book" or "try writing anything" on my various to-do lists, and then I sat most mornings helplessly at my computer for an hour or so before giving up. I'm prone to catastrophizing my problems, and more than a few times I worried that I had frittered away the very last gasps of my writing life on promotional copy.

Usually winter and summer breaks from teaching are extraordinarily productive times for me, but over that winter break of 2018–2019, I continued to write nothing at all. What finally broke me out of my slump was that just before the start of the new semester, a beloved former student emailed to ask me how to get over writer's block. I had to tell them something, so I first recycled all the usual advice about freewriting and writing to prompts and so on. Then I added: sometimes it helps to give yourself arbitrary constraints. Simplify the task by eliminating some of the variables.

I believe in the advice I give to students, but I am often too dense or stubborn to apply it to my own work; this was a rare moment where I listened. After spending some time thinking of possible constraints I could impose on myself, I settled on a project guided by the following rules:

- Write an essay for every year you've been alive
- Each one should be a maximum of 1,500 words, preferably closer to 1,000
- No/minimal research (this was self-preservation, knowing that otherwise I would end up spending 12 hours read-

ing random newspaper articles from 1986 and calling it writing)

- Every essay should broaden out to something bigger than just the self or a single incident
- Write in order, chronologically
- Write a draft of a new essay in one sitting, one per day

I broke the final two rules almost immediately; the first piece I wrote was "1988," because I vividly remembered the monorail at the Philadelphia Zoo falling off the tracks while I was there (and anyway I had no ideas for 1982 at all). I finished the first draft in an hour; it ended up in a totally different place from where I'd expected to go, and I felt excited about writing for the first time in a couple years. The next day, I wrote another (1994), and the next day another (2006). I didn't stay on that pace, breaking the last rule, but within two months, I had 37 essay drafts completed.

The constraint of the word count—an arbitrary number, a number low enough to prevent me from getting bogged down in the asides and unnecessary explanations to which I'm prone—forced me to make choices I would not otherwise make. Early on, I was still overwriting, finishing drafts at 1,900 or 2,400 words and then having to make dramatic cuts to get beneath the limit. The easiest cuts were at the ends of paragraphs, where I was always adding two or three sentences over-explaining myself, holding the reader's hand. As the project progressed, I found myself making the cuts naturally before even typing them; once I had a sense of the rhythms of these pieces, I more instinctively flowed from one idea to the next, eschewing the labored transitions that strangle all my early drafts. I had to learn to trust the work to speak for itself, even when shifting time and place within the space of a paragraph. It was this freedom of movement that ultimately gave the project life. I was deep under the spell of books by Denis Johnson (*The Largesse of the Sea Maiden*) and Alejandro Zambra (*My Documents*) at the time I was drafting this book; two very different writers from me, and from each other, but also two writers with the confidence and audacity to tell stories that appear at first glance to be meandering and plotless, while in fact being precisely and beautifully structured.

By beginning with the basic constraints of years and word count, and mostly sticking to the no-research rule (I admit to doing quick searches to confirm specific dates of incidents, as well as some conspicuous Wikipedia browsing and digging through my mom's photo albums for inspiration on the first five years), I was able to free myself to write in a voice that felt authentic to me but also surprising. I had the experience you want when writing memoir—starting on one topic and discovering halfway through that you're actually writing about something completely different. The goal was to produce pieces where the constraint wouldn't be noticeable unless someone pointed it out; to be free and fluid but also highly controlled. This is not unlike the way I try to appear laid back and spontaneous among friends while actually being a tightly wound bundle of anxieties. Writing is a performance, after all. Especially when you're writing about yourself.

Since that initial batch, I have added five more pieces, each one in the spirit of the originals. I don't know if I'll continue producing these, but I like having this project, having the accountability of saying at least one meaningful thing about each year. (Have I personally discovered journaling? Did I invent this?) There's no way of documenting it all, but it has been a surprisingly profound and challenging exercise to try to get something on the page. To decide what to prioritize and when. To see which ideas emerge over and over no matter what I'm planning on writing about. And, when it came time to compile them all into a single manuscript, to see how I could highlight some of these recurring ideas, to draw connections between them, to stitch each individual piece into a more coherent whole. In some ways, these connections made themselves; whatever people and events and anxieties were preoccupying me continually found their way onto the page. I want a reader to be able to flip to a random essay in here and feel it's complete, but I also want the essays to accumulate and build on each other for the reader who proceeds chronologically. I want the reader to feel the weight of each mounting year the same way I have. This is not my whole life, but it's close enough. It's certainly more than anyone needs to know.

—*Tom McAllister*

It All Felt Impossible

1982

The Commodore 64 was launched in the year I was born and went on to become the best-selling single computer model of all time; we wouldn't own the Commodore ourselves until four or five years later, at which point it would become one of the focal points of my and my brother's lives. I'm trying to write an essay for every year I've been alive, and I started my research on this year by checking Wikipedia. I know most facts on the internet are at least a little bit false, but if you've been online as long as I have, you learn how to sort through all the competing lies and assemble the world you prefer, like wild birds building their nests from gold foil and bright plastics and other especially striking bits of trash. Besides, most of the facts I know about my own life are at least a little bit false. Whatever I tell you about the first six years especially can't be trusted.

The Wikipedia page for 1982 also includes many details about the Falklands War, a war I am familiar with only because of *The Simpsons* episode "Burns' Heir," in which Krusty the Clown interrupts his show with breaking news that the Falklands have just been invaded. I still barely know anything about the Falklands War except that I make it a policy to be skeptical of the group with the biggest guns, the thickest body armor, the most money. Throughout my childhood, imperial Western powers were fussing with the lives of people in South America and North Africa. They were deposing and installing leaders according to their idiosyncratic whims. They were brutally murdering dissidents. They were lying about it all and pretending to be liberators. We're living in an era of great blowback now; the crimes of my parents' generation have resulted

1

in the irreversible destruction of the planet, a horrifying refugee crisis for which no one will take responsibility, and the rise of fascism throughout the Western world. I was not concerned about colonialism then; I focused mostly on consumption and excretion. You can't blame me for this. A baby's curiosity only extends so far.

When you're a baby, you're not thinking about terrorism or rising sea levels or the destruction of coral reefs. You're thinking about your mother's face, latching on to that familiar sight that makes you smile, and as a result, makes her smile, no matter how tired she is. You are a source of constant joy, except when you're not. Your mom loves you so much and you've done nothing to deserve it, and you will spend a lifetime trying to prove you're worthy. The Falklands have been invaded. You are hungry. It's all happening at the same time.

Though I did comparatively very little in 1982, it is fair to note here that one thing I did do was emerge, a living being, from my mother's womb. I grew and learned to smile and began to crawl and ate solid foods and sprouted nubs of teeth from inside my own skull. My mom says I was a good baby. I was her second son, but, I learned many years later, not her second pregnancy. Women were having miscarriages all the time, but nobody talked about it. Women have to live two lives, one in public and one in private; if these lives intersect, that's when men start to get angry.

There is a picture of me at one month old, being held by my grandfather—the war hero, the man who personally killed a dozen Nazis in a single morning. My dad's father was already dead, due to complications from alcoholism. My mom's father would be dead soon too: colon cancer. I was named after both of them, and legally I am Walter Thomas, though my parents always called me Tom, a minor discrepancy I find myself explaining to anyone who reads my name on an official form. Sometimes friendly strangers behind desks will call me Walt and I won't respond because I forget it's my name. For some reason when I was in sixth grade people started taunting me by chanting the name *Walter* and for some reason it made me so angry that I tackled one of my best friends in the school parking lot and had every intention of smashing his face into the asphalt had I not been restrained. The things that can upset you when you're young are so stupid, but that doesn't make them any less upsetting.

The 1982 edition of *Best American Short Stories* includes a story by James Ferry memorably titled "Dancing Ducks and Talking Anus." It is the only story he ever published. The way academia worked then, he could have gotten a tenured job in an MFA program somewhere if he'd just published two more stories. Then he could have squatted on that job for the next 35 years, maybe evolving and experimenting in his writing and his teaching, or maybe becoming a resentful, power-hoarding crank who never learned the names of his younger colleagues or updated his syllabus after 1991. I've been in academia for 21 years, on a series of one-year contracts at the same school (our provost recently sent a school-wide email encouraging us to "work together" as the school works to "right size" our faculty over the next five to seven years). The tenured faculty member in the office next to mine has spoken to me exactly one time, when he barged into my office and said, "Hey, you work here, right?" He's rude, but he is perceptive. He wanted me to agree with him that he was being unfairly accused of bullying his colleagues. He told me it was all bullshit and assumed I agreed. I nodded, and he left. He's very well respected in his field, which does not give him permission to treat people like shit. That's a simple concept a lot of people don't understand.

I think of James Ferry often, wondering what qualifies as writing success, and whether that one triumph of his was worth the years of frustration, rejection, uncertainty. By almost any measure, I have had a successful run as a writer. I've gone to a prestigious grad school, published three books and dozens of short stories and essays. Still, most days, when I check my email, I feel a little twinge somewhere deep in my soul, worrying that today is the day they're going to cut me off. Someone is going to write and tell me that, on behalf of all writers across the globe, I've been ordered to stop immediately. Time to step aside and let someone new have a shot.

This business is not a competition, but I forget that sometimes.

I've talked about all of this before—in my classes and on Twitter and on my podcast and to my wife and to myself. Even as I am accumulating new stories, I am mostly repeating the same old ones in perpetuity. It used to bother me at family gatherings when older relatives relayed the same stories they've told a hundred times, so we could all build to a familiar punchline and react as if it was the first time we'd ever heard it. As I get older, I am learning to appreciate the virtue of repetition, of revising our histories and trying again to view them in a new light. Had I encountered the story of James Ferry in my mid-twenties, just after grad school, I would have traveled down to the crossroads myself and sold my soul on the spot for a story in *Best American*. Now all I can think about is the harsh comedown from the acceptance and the blur of success. The way the rest of his writing life didn't measure up to what he might have expected.

There's one more fact here that I have to mention. 1982 is the year LauraBeth, my wife, was born. We didn't know each other then. She was a baby too, and babies only are allowed to know the people their parents or guardians introduce them to. We wouldn't meet for another 18 years, but is there any more important development in my life? Her birth is the event that shapes everything that follows. She wishes I wouldn't write about her so much, in so many different venues. But I don't know what else to write about. This is my life. She's the reason that, whatever happens in the interim, I am doing relatively okay. Which in itself is an achievement. You show up in this place one day, helpless, and for a long time you stay helpless, and the only thing you can do is find good people to lean on while you figure the rest out.

1983

I know from my mom's impressively detailed notes in my baby book that I started standing on my own in February. I know I started walking a month later. I know I took my first vacation—to Ocean City, Maryland—in June. By December, I was able to string together two to three words at a time, though it would be many years before I felt comfortable talking to anyone outside my home (until I was seven, I hid behind my parents' legs and barked at adults who spoke to me). These are all milestones about which I have almost nothing to say. Whatever I was doing or thinking during this time was of great importance to a handful of people, and none to anyone else. I would rather talk about what was on TV.

Like most American families, our living space was structured around the TV, so even if I wasn't watching myself, I knew its presence, found comfort in the sound of static as my parents fiddled with the antenna, tracked the wild colors bounding across the screen, felt the fine hairs on my arm standing up and reaching toward it. I was already being shaped by TV. We would have been watching sports most weekends: football on Sundays, baseball when my grandmother was around, maybe basketball (the 76ers won the NBA championship that year—two of their six Finals games broadcast on tape delay—the first Philly sports championship of my life and the only one until 2008, a long string of failures, frustrations, and bad luck that I would internalize and come to view as central to my own identity, not to mention the city's). I can safely assume that my parents—along with me and my older brother, Kevin—were among the 106 million people who watched the *M*A*S*H* finale. I would surely

5

have been sitting in my mom's arms as she turned on *Magnum, P.I.* and nurtured her lifelong devotion to Tom Selleck. Before I could walk, I would have seen a dozen or more episodes of *Hawaii Five-O.* Would have seen the Fonz pounding on a broken jukebox and making it whir back to life, would have been unable to follow the intrigue on *Dallas* but sensed something was wrong in the world. Over the next 17 years, I would spend more time in front of that TV than any other place, often with a copy of *TV Guide* in my lap, absorbing reruns of the shows that had been important to my parents and Kevin. Throughout my life, I have never prayed with much conviction or sincerity, but sometimes when I was young and stuck at church with my family, I knelt there and looked solemnly toward the altar and asked God to make my favorite shows real places I could visit. I would fantasize often about learning some magic incantation that would transport me inside the TV, not because I wanted to be a star but because I wanted to sit next to Cliff and Norm and laugh at Carla's jokes. To be a non-speaking extra at the Regal Beagle while Jack and Mr. Furley stumbled through another hilarious misunderstanding. To feel the heat of the explosions as the A-Team outmaneuvered another gang of local thugs. To maybe someday become friends with all these people I loved from a distance. I didn't comprehend any of the jokes in *Three's Company* until I was much older, but I understood that something funny was happening. I trusted the laugh track and I trusted the responses of the adults around me. Now, like everyone else, I am addicted to my phone; I spend all day mashing the screen to demand that it deliver me more sad and infuriating and unhealthy content. Now and then I look up and shake my head about how my nephew is addicted to his tablet. I feel, at times, more distant from the real world than I ever have. Every child absorbs the atmosphere in which they live. Don't ask me to explain the science. I took a Developmental Psychology course in college, but it's been a long time, and I trashed my textbooks last time we moved. I'm just trying to talk about how things *feel*.

1984

In the photographs from this time, the ashtrays are ubiquitous and ornate, and everyone is smoking. My grandmother smoked so much that the ceiling lining in her car sagged like a hammock (she'd once caught my mom stealing one of her cigarettes and made her eat it, a punishment that deterred her for life). Though my dad is the focus of very few pictures, he's often in the background or cut off by the edge, and you can see that he's holding a cigarette. He'd grown up spending his free time in pool halls, where I imagine he'd kept an unlit cigarette behind his ear while making low-stakes bets with his friends and hitting the kinds of impossible bank shots he used to sink when we played mini golf on vacation. He'd quit smoking when Kevin was born in 1976 and started again at some point before my birth. He would quit again a few years later, and I would think of him as a non-smoker for most of his life. He chewed on coffee stirrers as a substitute, some way to work out whatever tension smoking had once eased in him. Everywhere in the house, I found mangled coffee stirrers that had fallen out of his pockets. If an archaeologist excavated our house tomorrow, they'd find it was built on a foundation of coffee stirrers.

When he died of esophageal cancer, it may have just been bad luck. But he'd smoked for many years. The choices you make when you're a teenager matter in a way you cannot possibly imagine, no matter how often adults warn you about it. You can pretend not to understand the math, but it all adds up, with or without your permission.

I didn't learn until long after his death that he had started smoking again, periodically and surreptitiously. Cigars in the evening, after a stressful day of work as the manager at an office furniture warehouse. Maybe on those long nights when he stayed up past midnight watching TV, he was not hanging on every word of Jay Leno's monologue like we'd thought, but was waiting for us to finally fall asleep so that he could step outside onto our patio and have a cigar and feel normal again. To stop denying himself and live in a nicotine-rich moment. To think about nothing else besides the physical pleasure of poisoning yourself. He spent a minimum of 12 hours every day at work, plus an hour commute each way. He wanted to smoke. He knew by this point that smoking could kill him, had seen friends and relatives die from it. I bet smoking out there on the patio under the moon was one of the best feelings of his life. I bet he dreamed about it all afternoon, and in those brief moments, he allowed himself to think: *Let it kill me, it's worth it right now.* I bet he thought: *We're doing okay. We're gonna make it.*

Now I've slipped into writing fiction. In short stories people go outside and consider the stars and experience epiphanies all the time. In real life, sometimes people just want a cigarette and that's all there is to it. It's too easy to graft the artifice onto a few concrete details and impose meaning that isn't there. I don't know the circumstances of his smoking. I'm creating a character out of my dad because I can't say that I really knew or understood him. A large portion of my adulthood has been spent imagining the secret lives of my parents, the details that have been hidden from us not because they're scandalous but because they aren't remarkable enough to mention.

Most of what I know about him—now, 21 years after his death—is pieced together from my unreliable memories, Kevin's slightly stronger memories, and stories my mom has since told us. She's the one who told LauraBeth about the cigars, and about her frustration with him. In hindsight, I remember her being so angry when he was diagnosed with cancer, and then I didn't understand. I want to be angry at him too, but I can't do it. Your parents expend so much energy protecting you from all the dangers in the world, and they do most of it thanklessly.

In one of my novels, I end a chapter with this line: "Self-medicate whenever possible. Whatever drug is helping you to cope is one that will kill you but at least you're maintaining some control over how and when you go." Every time I read it in public, people laugh, which I did not expect. I have this problem where the things I think are funny are actually sad, and the things I think are depressing are actually funny. To me, the self-medication line is not a joke. There's a stigma against feeling pleasure for pleasure's sake. So I drink too much—I know this. Sometimes I feel great shame about it. Sometimes LauraBeth suggests it would be good to cut back. Sometimes I open one more beer even though I don't really want one, and then I open another after that. But sometimes it's a beautiful Wednesday afternoon and I can't imagine anything better than meeting my wife in the city for an outdoor happy hour and drinking a couple draft beers while we watch strangers streaming past us. I want to argue that there are pleasures in not solving problems too.

In 1984 there was a very famous television commercial for Apple Macintosh computers. I don't know why I have been subjected to dozens of viewings of this commercial and its so-called importance. It is, all things considered, a dumb commercial, and our insistence on treating advertising like art is one of the main sources of cultural rot in this country. This ad is an homage to a famous novel called 1984, a novel that people who don't read like to reference any time they dislike the passage of a new law. A specific type of person loves referencing 1984 when they get criticized for saying something racist or sexist or otherwise cruel. TV pundits are especially fond of broadly referencing Orwell, of describing developments as Orwellian, and trusting that you know this means they are very smart indeed and they went to good schools. Excluding religious texts, it's possible that 1984 is the book that the most people pretend to have read. If you create something famous enough, eventually it will become so ubiquitous that all of its meanings flatten into nothingness. I could say my dad's desire to smoke was Orwellian, and if I said this with enough confidence, you would have to believe me. Who cares what it means? They invented meaning just to fuck with us.

1985

My mom notes in the baby book that I celebrated my third birthday at Chuck E. Cheese, and received the following gifts: He-Man figures, GoBots, blocks, and a Fisher-Price tape recorder. The next year I received G.I. Joes. The year after, it was more G.I. Joes, a couple Transformers, and some kind of gun. It's normal in America to give guns to boys. It's normal when children are young enough that they're still learning how to use a toilet ("urine toilet trained," my mom notes in 1985), to give them a pile of army men and let them figure it all out on their own. It's normal to play by pretending to kill people over and over again. These gifts are the beginning of an indoctrination into a culture of celebrating gun violence, of blithely accepting that cops and troops are good guys and that the bad guys are anyone they say is bad. It's almost understandable that this relentless messaging would lead to the election of Donald Trump, one of the world's most unpleasant and superficial men, a textbook coward who likes troops because they get to carry guns and drive big tanks and scowl at people. Other, smarter people have already written about all of this. You don't need me to explain how the concept of masculinity is poisoned from birth. The evidence is right there if you google it. It's on you to do the required reading.

Early in a recent semester, I tried to get my students to consider the ways in which conventional performances of masculinity are harmful not just to women but to the men who are doing the performing. I asked them to think of times when playing a traditionally masculine role has gotten them, or people they know, into trouble. To spur conversation, I told them about a time when my soccer teammates and I had gotten into a brawl during a game because the opposing team's fans kept mocking us for wearing effeminate purple jerseys (we won the game but got kicked out of the tournament). The students gave me blank stares, though that's not unusual for an 8 AM Freshman Comp course. Everyone is just trying to survive and waiting on the keywords from me to unlock the secret to a good grade. Even the most diligent students have bigger priorities than my course. They've also by now heard bits and pieces of this kind of discussion before—if not in a classroom, then on TikTok or Tumblr—so they can parrot the term "toxic masculinity" if I require them to. They might be annoyed because they believe they already know all this stuff. They might also understand they only have a small part of it figured out, and they're afraid of being wrong out loud. You can reassure students that being wrong in the right space is the whole key to learning, but that doesn't make it any less stressful. So I went back to the text (a scholarly study of male group behaviors in ESPN Zone sports bars, a reading I personally found pretty interesting though very few students agreed). I showed them the quotable lines. I talked about how one could write an essay about this topic. I hoped that for at least a few of them, progress was made.

After class, one guy approached me to talk about the day's discussion—he's quiet, but he listens—and he said, in his thick Brooklyn accent, an accent so exaggerated it sounds like one a bad actor would use in a commercial for frozen bagels: "I don't know about all that, you know, masculinity stuff? It's like... aren't we all just animals? We're just being the way animals are? Like when you're watching TV and there's a lioness walking around and whatnot, and then there's the lion behind her. Then the fucking Australian guy starts talking about mating or whatever. You know?" I'm pretty sure he was high, but he was there and he was working on it. We carried the conversation into the hall and down the stairs and out toward the center of campus, like a professor and student in the movies. Because he never turned anything in on time, I didn't know if he was going to pass the class, but I liked him, and I liked the weird energy he added to our room. Conversations like this one are among the highlights of my life these days. In pushing a student to grope clumsily toward a new understanding of the world, I feel like I'm doing something worthwhile; I feel like I have a chance to redirect them toward a way of thinking and living that is one percent better than the way they're thinking and living now. The concept of fun means a totally different thing for me than it did 40 years ago. I've lost or destroyed all those toys I got when I was a kid. I don't think about He-Man at all now. When I was three, I couldn't have imagined anything more important.

1986

The first real memory I can genuinely pinpoint by year is the arrival of a puppy named Maggie, a white mutt with a black patch of fur around her left eye. My grandmother's dog had whelped a litter and the puppies needed to be placed with new owners. Between the eyepatch and the studio-ready scruffiness, Maggie looked like she could have been the star of a moderately successful live-action kids' movie. Maybe something where she joins a Little League team as a pinch runner, or one where she helps some plucky kids stop the scheming mayor from bulldozing the laser tag arena.

One of my favorite pictures of myself (I tend to cringe at pictures of myself, though anyone who doesn't do this sometimes should not be trusted) is of me and Maggie sitting together inside the cardboard box that acted as her temporary shelter. There is an unfiltered joy on my face, a slightly mischievous smile. What I love about the picture is that it's such a clear indicator of how I will behave for the rest of my life. Though I will overanalyze nearly every human interaction the moment it ends, I will gravitate instinctively to all animals. This will become one of my defining characteristics for anyone who knows me even casually. A couple years ago, an acquaintance told me she used to be intimidated by me, thought I was surly and judgmental, but when she saw my frequent social media posts about dogs—mine, my friends', my neighbors'—she thought I might actually be nice. "You want people to think you're mean," she said, "But you're not." I told her not to let the secret out; there are some perks to people thinking the worst of you.

Maggie chewed on furniture and pooped in the house and vomited with seemingly no cause and at least once got caught in the glue traps meant for the mice. I remember her yelping and stomping around, the trap flapping on her foot like a scuba flipper. Neither of my parents had the patience to deal with a hyperactive puppy, and my brother and I were too young to be helpful. She was gone before we knew anything about her (Maggie was technically not my first dog; the first was Winston, an English bulldog who my mom loved deeply, but who she had to send away to an [actual] farm because he was so jealous of me that he tried to eat me, or at least chew on me a little bit).

A few years later, we got another dog, a black lab/collie mix whose hip was broken when she was hit by a car. She'd belonged to one of my mom's co-workers, who had a newborn and didn't have the energy or time to care for an injured dog. Buttons slept in a crate in the basement until she healed, and I spent long hours sitting next to the crate, talking to her, because I didn't want her to be alone and afraid. Many years later, after I started dating LauraBeth, she would tell me about how, around the same age, she used to sleep on the floor next to the cage that contained their golden retriever puppy, Chipper. One of the foundational elements of our relationship is our shared love of animals. We're both more likely to trust another person if we find they also love animals the way we do.

I'm getting way ahead of myself. In the interim there are long nights when Buttons is terrified by thunder and barges into my room whimpering and I try to comfort her. There is Holly, the border collie up the street who I stop to pet every day on the way to and from my bus stop. There is Grunt, the guinea pig whose sudden death I mourn by working with my dad to make a memorial on our Lite-Brite board. There is my aunt's dog Max, who spins in manic circles and urinates every time someone enters the house. There are the many wild animals (a reindeer, a polar bear, two whales) that are "adopted" for me as gifts. I can't list for you every pet I've known and loved because there's not enough room here. Right now on my phone there are pictures of 26 dogs: dogs I have owned, dogs I have walked for friends, dogs I have met at parties, dogs I have met on vacation, dogs belonging to neighbors, and one dog who is actually a plush animal that I've owned for 20 years. On my computer, there are 10 more dogs, at least. I could draw you a map of all the dogs in town. I consider all these dogs to be my friends. I have maintained a comprehensive knowledge of their lineages and their personality quirks, details I keep to myself because I understand nobody else is interested in hearing about it.

I have never felt close to the same level of enthusiasm for knowing my own family history or maintaining long-term relationships with most people. I always say I have a small family, but that's not really true; my mom has 11 aunts and uncles, and, between them and everyone on my dad's side, I have hundreds of cousins, most of whom still live in the Philly area. When I was growing up, no matter where we drove in the city, I could count on my mom pointing out the window and saying, "That guy over there is your cousin." For a brief period, two of those cousins lived under the same bridge at the same time but didn't realize they were related. My Uncle Jim maintains extensive records of our family trees, sometimes sending messages to let me know he's discovered old pictures of Aunt Somebody or Cousin Whoever. In theory, I would like to have access to this information, to the tragic and comic stories of our family's past. From a purely selfish perspective, it would give me more stories to write about. But when my mom tells me about the wedding of a cousin I may have met once in 1986, I forget all the details immediately. When my Uncle Jim narrates the history of some distant Duffy relative, I realize I am not really listening, though a part of me knows I probably should be listening. Digging through photo albums to brainstorm for this project, I see so many older relatives whose names I do not know and will never make the effort to learn. My tenuous connections to family through Facebook do nothing to enhance my life or knowledge of myself.

I have stressed to my family that I do not want them to buy me one of those ancestry DNA kits as a gift, but I'm afraid one day they'll run out of ideas and do it anyway. Besides being skeptical of the science, and especially disliking the way people use their results to make weird and uncomfortable comments about race (an acquaintance: "I found out I'm 6% Nigerian; I always knew I had some Black blood in me"), I can't imagine how the results would mean anything to me. I realize I might have more interest if I had an ambiguous ethnic background, or if my ancestors had been dragged to this country against their will, or if they'd fled here to escape persecution. I don't know how it would change my perspective on anything to get math involved. I don't like thinking about numbers for very long. I'd much rather dump a huge pile of words in your lap and after you sort through them, you'll have a much better chance of figuring out who I am. The answer is in here somewhere. If it's not, then I don't know where I'm supposed to look.

1987

I have this incredibly vivid memory of being young and walking with my grandmother and my parents along Main Street in Manayunk, the Philly neighborhood where both my parents grew up. It's a warm summer day and we're going to Overbrook Water Ice, one of my favorite places in the world (someone later told me it was a drug front, but I can't find any evidence that's true, and now that I examine it some more I realize there's a good chance this rumor started because it was the only Black-owned business in the neighborhood). I'm stomping on the metal cellar doors in the sidewalk outside every storefront, and my parents are warning me not to do it, and I keep clanking anyway, and then one swings open like a trap door and I plummet into a strange basement. I am injured and terrified. Adults scramble to piece me back together again.

This memory flashes into my mind every time I'm walking through a city, watching people recklessly step onto these doors, thinking about how the sidewalk is littered with gaping holes, tombs for the careless. If crowding forces me to step on one, I try to skip lightly across the surface as if running on hot coals. I imagine myself each time plummeting into an underworld from which there is no escape, hot and full of hissing steam pipes and ruled by sewer trolls (it's possible I'm picturing the Negative World from *Super Mario Bros.*; it's possible I'm only capable of conjuring nightmares based on entertainments). I have frequently told friends and acquaintances about this traumatic moment from my past.

But it couldn't have happened. My parents have no memory of it, for one thing. For another, those doors are designed to swing out, not drop in, to avoid exactly the accident I have always feared. I have no scars or other evidence of the type of injury that would accompany the fall, and I know I broke my first bone at 12 and got my first stitches at 20. There would have been doctors and lawyers and lawsuits.

Then why do I remember it so well? Did I invent this memory in a dream, or was it planted there by my parents' dire warnings? Isn't the most important thing that this fear has dictated my behaviors for years? This was a formative experience, whether it happened or not.

I can try all I want to be as truthful as possible, but I have no way to verify most of the information I'm sharing. They are events I remember having occurred, and that I can describe in great detail. Still, I need to acknowledge that it's possible that some (most?) of the stories I've told to friends over the years have been invented, in whole or part. What I really want to know is: can fears, if felt deeply and intensely enough, generate these experiences in our minds? What is the difference between me having actually fallen and me feeling absolutely certain that I have fallen?

Another memory: I'm at my grandmother's house, a few years after I did not fall through the cellar door, and it is trash day. Her dog, Patches (a shepherd mix), has died. My grandmother is stoic, but I know she is very sad. Later that day, we are watching *Davy Crockett: King of the Wild Frontier* and I am wearing my beloved coonskin cap. When Davy dies at the Alamo, I ask why he had to die. My question is literally about the movie, as in why would they kill off the hero instead of letting him win? But she thinks the question is about death in general, and she enumerates the reasons God calls people's souls into heaven. I regret having asked the question, because I know that evening my dad will sit me down at the kitchen table and have a serious talk with me about death and dying. He will ask me to articulate my own vision of the afterlife and explain how I've come to these conclusions. He will not let me go to bed until I've given him real and substantial answers.

When we leave her house, I see that Patches has been stuffed into a cardboard box on the curb. The box has tipped over and Patches' head lolls out the side onto the sidewalk. I stare into her dead dog eyes and I feel a dread I will never forget. I can close my eyes right now and visualize the dog's face. I have written this image into a half-dozen failed short stories. I'm putting it here in hopes of finally removing it from my brain.

Again, there's no way this event could have happened as I remember it. Wikipedia tells me that Crockett doesn't even die in the movie (though his death is described as "inevitable"). It is extremely unlikely that the death of Patches occurred on the same day as the Davy Crockett incident (though your mind likes events to be orderly, likes to combine events that have no business being combined). And, most importantly, why would my grandmother, a devout Catholic who harbored a deep respect for God's creation, throw a dog into a cardboard box? Why would nobody address the dog in the box with me, but spend time gauging my feelings on the Alamo?

Here's one more: I'm in the backseat of my grandmother's car and there is a hole rusted into the floor beneath my feet. As we drive through Philly running errands for her church, I stare into the hole, watching the asphalt whiz beneath us. At a red light, I try to work up the courage to reach my foot down through the hole to the street. Before I do it, the light changes and we're rolling again. Every couple minutes, I let my foot dangle above the hole and consider jamming it through like Fred Flintstone, just to see what will happen. Imagination is overall a good quality, but sometimes it can get you killed.

It goes without saying that this also couldn't have happened as I remember it. Car safety standards were more lax, but my grandmother was a careful person. My parents wouldn't have let me ride in a car without a floor. Yet just this week I sat in the back seat of a friend's car and when I pressed my foot down to the mat, the memory of that hole flashed back in perfect detail, and I felt that sensation of being inches from getting sucked into another dimension. There are holes everywhere, and you never know what's at the bottom of them until you dive in.

Does the fear create the memory or does the memory create the fear? This country is sick with nostalgia for a forgotten, lost America, but most of the features people love about that America never existed in the first place. Politicians paint vivid portraits of a great America just beyond our grasp, and even accounting for the way these narratives whitewash history and represent a longing for a return of racial segregation and traditional gender norms, it's strange to think about how much of our understanding of the country's golden age comes from *Grease* and reruns of *Happy Days* and visits to kitschy diners. Every cherished entertainment turns into propaganda eventually. Most of the far-right organizers and militias forming online are very young; they have been told their whole lives that just a generation before they were born, this place was a utopia. It's all predicated on invented histories. Their fury is a fear of losing something they never had in the first place.

1988

In September, my grandmother took me to the zoo. My favorite animals then were the two polar bears, which on cool days you could watch lounging on the rocks or playing with toys that looked like ultra-durable beach balls, but the real treat was to stand at the lower level and observe through the glass when they dove underwater. Each dive created a frenzy of overstimulated children pounding on the glass, shrieking and trying to get the bear to make eye contact. It must have been a nightmare for the bears. They had gouged a network of scratches into every inch of the glass on the inside. At the time, I believed it was a sign they were trying to escape, and I wondered if they dreamed of breaking out and killing us.

One of the bears was a female named Coldilocks. She was transferred as a cub from the Seneca Park Zoo in Rochester, New York to Philly in 1981 and lived until 2018, euthanized at age 37, the oldest polar bear in captivity. Given the planet's decline, she may well have been the oldest polar bear most of us will ever see. Coldilocks had never experienced life in the wild, but there is too much evolutionary history for it not to have been coded into her genes. There had to have been a longing, always, for some other life that she couldn't quite identify. I'm often guilty of anthropomorphizing animals; I want small moments to be loaded with hidden meaning so that my own life feels consequential. It's possible she was happy to have a comfortable place to sleep, some water to swim in, and another bear to socialize with. Regular feedings. No dangers besides disease. My understanding is that the average zoo animal does not consider escape because it is so far removed from its habitat that anything

22

outside the enclosure is alien and sinister. Still, it's hard to know how to feel about zoo animals, who are living a definitively unnatural life while also performing this important educational and fundraising function. During a period of professional crisis eight years ago—I had lost faith in the institution of higher education and in my role in perpetuating it—I applied for two marketing and development jobs at the zoo. I didn't get an interview, and I didn't tell LauraBeth until after the crisis had (mostly) passed. She thought I was joking at first, then she asked, "How do you know you wouldn't hate that job even more?" But the lingering part of me that once dreamed of being a marine biologist thought, *at least I'd be doing something useful.*

I presume the zookeepers never told Coldilocks that the polar ice caps are melting at alarming rates, or that her native ecosystem appears to be on the verge of total collapse. Even if she had been allowed to watch the news every evening, she would have still been ignorant, would have learned mostly about daily weather forecasts and inspirational cops and the sexual indiscretions of famous people, because the national media has never treated the climate crisis seriously, and has portrayed activists as naïve or hypocritical or insane. She never would have seen the viral videos of emaciated polar bears stumbling to their death in sweltering conditions. She would never know a single thing outside the boundaries of her pen. She's dead now, but when I started this project she was alive and the same age as me; every writerly impulse in my brain wants me to make this a metaphor for something, but there are so many differences between me and a polar bear.

As my grandmother and I stood by the penguin enclosure that afternoon, we felt the ground shake beneath us. Within seconds, sirens wailed, and people began running, confused, in all directions. My grandmother pulled me aside and calmly waited to determine what had happened. If it were 2023, I would have assumed an active shooter was rampaging through the zoo, but that's not a threat we worried about then. "Active shooter" wasn't even a term anyone knew, wouldn't be used in any format for another decade.

We would soon learn that the monorail—the first monorail ever at any zoo—had fallen off the tracks. This was the third monorail incident at the zoo in a two-year period. There had been an electrical fire in May, and before that there was another accident with an unclear cause. I have found one message board devoted to Philly nostalgia in which a poster insists the 1988 accident was caused by two teenagers having sex on the monorail, but I'm not sure how sex causes monorail crashes, and I've found no other sources corroborating this story.

I assume the tremors made the day traumatic for most of the animals, while it was mostly a curiosity for me. As the emergency vehicles sped past, my grandmother unfolded the map of the zoo and showed me where we were, then asked where I'd like to go next, as if we were in no danger at all. She pointed to the small red cross on the map to show me where medical and emergency services were located. "This is where people like your mom work," she said. "She makes sick people better." This is a fundamental truth I have understood about my mom for my whole life.

One afternoon, while my mom drove Kevin to his guitar lesson, we were waiting at a red light on Ridge Avenue and saw a man collapse on the corner, hitting his head on the sidewalk. In my memory, she shifted into park in the middle of the road and hopped out of the car. She tells me now that her first impulse was to keep on driving, but Kevin looked at her and said, "Mom, you're a nurse, shouldn't you help?" She felt guilted into pulling over. Kevin ran to call 911 while I stayed in the car. I lost sight of my mom in the crowd that had gathered. Thanks to TV, I assumed she was down on her knees performing chest compressions and breathing life back into his lungs, though I know it was all less dramatic than that; she says there were already three ICU nurses on the scene, so she stood by for a minute and then left him in their care. The man had collapsed due to low blood sugar, and we were only a couple blocks from Roxborough Memorial, my mom's hospital. My mom was wearing a shirt with a pattern of tiny swinging monkeys on it. I cannot explain why that's the detail I remember most clearly. The next day, while making her rounds with the IV Team, she found the fallen man, and learned he was going to be fine. When she tells this story now, she emphasizes her reluctance to help, downplays her desire to check on him later (she often says she and I are the same person, apologizes to LauraBeth for it).

I know and am related to a lot of people who work in the health-care field, and they have collectively seen so many people die that their understanding of the tragic is different from most people's. They have this remarkable ability to convert a physical catastrophe into a series of protocols and procedures, with specific ends in mind. When people talk about first responders, they revert to clichés about bravery and sacrifice, but it's pragmatism. They know how the systems work, and they let their bodies take over. They have a sense of confidence that I feel about almost nothing, besides (sometimes) writing sentences. What looks superhuman is extreme competence. It doesn't make for an exciting montage, but maybe if our movies celebrated heroism as the culmination of a life of patient and thoughtful practice, rather than random miracles performed by angry men, we would be an overall healthier society.

Five years after the monorail accident, the famous *Simpsons* episode about defective monorails further confirmed for me that these machines are death traps, and I was too afraid to ride the monorail at the zoo before it was decommissioned in 2006. I finally rode a monorail in Seattle with LauraBeth two decades later and found it to be a perfectly fine way to get around, assuming you don't want to go too far, too fast. The Seattle monorail runs from a mall to the Space Needle and back. From the top of the Space Needle, looking out over Puget Sound and Mount Rainier, you can convince yourself that the world is as vast and beautiful as you've always wanted it to be. From inside the mall, you can get an Auntie Anne's pretzel for two bucks. The only thing separating these two experiences is a single elevated rail.

1989

Because film used to be so expensive, and photographs used to be a finite resource, almost every picture from my youth comes from birthdays and holidays. I have evidence, then, that I dressed as Destro, the international arms trader from *G.I. Joe*, for Halloween three years in a row. I have evidence that in 1989 I sat on a Fourth of July parade float with some other kids, and we obviously had no help in decorating it, having drawn bulky bubble letters that say, "PRESERVE our LIBERTY" in red and blue. I sat on a float in a Christmas parade that year too, wearing a shepherd's costume stitched by my grandmother, and by the end of that year I felt very strongly that parades are boring. Parades are relics from a time when people had no other means of entertainment or sharing news. Now they're good for keeping kids occupied a while, and for selling hot chocolate to raise funds for the PTA.

This is also the first year when I was allowed to invite friends to my birthday party (one of the last notes in my baby book lists friends who attended my fifth birthday two years earlier as, "Kevin, cousins, grandmom"). My seventh birthday party was at my favorite restaurant, Pizza Hut. We spent a while at the playground next door and then we went inside to eat. My mom made me go to the bathroom to wash my hands, and, I want to emphasize as strenuously as possible, the next three minutes are imprinted on my mind forever: in a rush to return to my friends, I squirted several pumps of soap onto my hands and tried to leave without rinsing them, but my hands were so slippery I couldn't turn the doorknob, and after a few tries I became frantic, first kicking the door and then pound-

26

ing on it with my fists, and then trying the slippery knob again, and then screaming. I was convinced they would forget about me and leave me in the bathroom. Every part of my mind that was capable of solving problems shut down, and I punched the door again; it swung open seconds later, thanks to another customer. The door was not locked. I'd never been trapped. Nobody had even noticed I was gone because it had been a normal amount of time for me to have been gone. I returned to the table, hands slick with soap. Whatever we did the rest of the day is long forgotten. I never told my parents about my bathroom scare.

My personal history is littered with these moments—of intense despair, certainty regarding my doom—that turned out to be harmless, exaggerated. The more time I spend writing about my youth, the more I realize how much my story is one of irrational panics. Moments of self-inflicted hysterics that dictate choices I make for the rest of my life. The gradual boxing in of my possibilities due to fears I have invented whole cloth. This is the same year when I tried to ride a bike with my friends, couldn't figure out how to stop, and crashed into a neighbor's garage while screaming, "Where's the brakes?" I left my bike behind and ran home and vowed never to get on a bike again (there are dozens of episodes like this in my youth, where one bad experience, even the hint of a bad experience, causes me to preemptively cut a simple pleasure out of my life forever). This is the same year my report card from my swim instructor at the YMCA said, "Tom has worked hard... he needs to continue to develop his confidence."

A psychologist might tell me there is a valuable lesson to learn from these new insights. But isn't life all about the urgency of the moment? Would I even be myself if I didn't get swept up in these waves of negativity, only to eventually find my footing and regroup? It's reassuring, in a way, to know that most crises eventually reveal themselves to be not crises at all. But: some problems are smaller than they appear at first. Some will never go away. If I'm not vigilant, how will I know when to panic and when to laugh?

On a Saturday afternoon, Kevin and his friends gathered in the living room to watch a VHS of *RoboCop*, the famous movie about the robot cop. They had rented it from West Coast Video, one of three video rental stores in the area; eventually two of those stores would turn into tanning salons, and then Blockbuster was king. The tanning salons died and then Blockbuster died, and for a while all three storefronts were empty. Today, they are, respectively: a dry cleaner, a pizza place, and a wine-tasting room. In the interim, the Blockbuster had been a Boston Market, and on its opening weekend, people lined up around the block, waiting an hour or more for a facsimile of a homecooked meal. I'd never seen so much enthusiasm for chicken. I first realized I was getting old when I started reciting the histories of various properties around town, expecting younger people to care that the vape shop used to be an ice cream shoppe, and that used to be a dog groomer, and so on. I distinctly remember not caring about this genre of story when I was young. I could argue that each closure is a small death, but it's not all that dramatic. West Coast Video closed because people like me stopped walking up there on Saturdays to rent old pro wrestling specials and peek through the beaded curtain into the adult section. Blockbuster died because the internet killed it. It does no one any good to get sentimental about old stores.

Kevin is six years older than I am; at this age I wanted desperately to hang with him and his friends, while they were just old enough to want nothing to do with me. Because I was only seven, I wasn't allowed to watch *RoboCop*, the famous movie about the robot cop. It had originally been given an X rating due to its hyperviolence, an incredible feat considering how much violence is allowed in PG-13 movies. The parent's guide on IMDB.com describes the most graphic sexual scene: "There is a scene in which two thugs are attempting to rape a young woman. One thug begins to rip off her clothes. RoboCop arrives and stops the rape from happening by shooting the thug's genitals." I sat at the top of the stairs, pretending I was part of the group and listening to the sound of gun-shots and screams and robotic clanking, and fumed over not being trusted to watch it too. Probably I heard a would-be rapist getting shot in the genitals by a robot cop; I would have had a hard time grasping most of that. Many years later, when I finally watched *RoboCop*, I realized that the movie is meant to satirize militarized policing and the media fixation on violence, but neither the movie's biggest fans nor its sequels seemed aware of or interested in the original intent. Surely, when I was seven, I wouldn't have seen anything but big guns and lots of blood. Within the next few years, I witnessed hundreds of on-screen murders and committed thousands more in various video games. Is it too obvious for me to point out how destructive it is, culturally, to be raised on entertainment built exclusively around heroic men murdering people? I mean—look around. Ask a cop in full SWAT gear if they understand Paul Verhoeven was mocking them with his little movie.

While I was writing the first draft of this essay, Donald Trump was pardoning a Navy SEAL who has been accused of the extrajudicial torture and murder of Iraqi teens, a man who was described by fellow SEALs as monstrous and out of control. A State Representative from California went on the radio to defend that SEAL by bragging about how he himself had probably killed hundreds of civilians when he was deployed. One of my old soccer teammates worked special ops in Afghanistan and later became a mercenary for Blackwater. The last time I saw him, he bragged about how easy it was to kill anyone you wanted over there. He died in 2020—either from Covid or an overdose, depending who you believe—and the *Inquirer* wrote a long article about how we had lost an American hero. The soldier is a good guy and the citizens are bad guys, and that's the full extent of our government policy. If they make a movie about this pardoned SEAL someday, it will be about the redemption of the criminal soldier, showing all the complex emotions he felt as he committed war crimes. If they wait long enough, they can make it a slapstick comedy. The victims barely exist, except as foils for the heroes.

1990

It was me, my 14-year-old brother Kevin, our Uncle Mike, and 19,301 other people in the Philadelphia Spectrum for SummerSlam 1990, and Rick Rude was standing at the top of the steel cage, blood flowing down his forehead. His manager, Bobby Heenan, shouted for him to turn and climb out of the cage to win the match, but wrestling logic dictated that he jump back in for one final attack on the Ultimate Warrior. Rude was one of the most famous heels in wrestling history (he had begun this match by taking the microphone and demanding silence from all of us "fat, out-of-shape Pennsylvania pissants," while he disrobed to reveal his oily body and tights with his own face airbrushed over the crotch). The Warrior, who was the babyface and the defending champ, countered his move, punching him in the stomach, marking the turn toward the inevitable: the good guy wins again, and we leap and scream along with everyone else as he celebrates with his championship belt, his iconic rocking theme music blaring through the arena. This is easily the fondest memory I have of my Uncle Mike, who I last saw when he was picking up a box of my deceased father's pants and my mom wouldn't let him in the house for reasons I have never known.

I took pro wrestling very seriously—much more seriously than Kevin, who has always been more capable than me of enjoying something without obsessing over it—and had already begun spending my allowance on wrestling video rentals and the latest issues of *Wrestling Observer*, *Wrestling News*, and *Pro Wrestling Illustrated*. I had been told repeatedly that it was scripted, but I was too invested in the mythology to care. Like many kids then, my hero was Hulk Hogan, who that night beat Earthquake in a grudge match that included some ringside interference from "The World's Strongest Man" Dino Bravo.

A few years later, Dino Bravo was murdered in his Quebec home, in a case long rumored to be mafia related. Earthquake died of heart failure not long after that. Rick Rude died of a drug overdose. Ultimate Warrior became infamous for his bizarre public persona and bigotry and conspiracy theorizing, and then he died unexpectedly. Hulk Hogan is still alive but has spent the past two decades embroiled in controversies involving secret sex tapes and ugly divorces and racist comments. Of the 35 in-ring performers I watched that night, 19 are dead, with an average age of death of 53 (a number inflated by two managers who were already in their 50s at the time of the show). About a third of the survivors have endured public struggles with addiction. It's normal for the entertainers of your youth to die off eventually, but the attrition rate in wrestling is especially high.

I have since read 14 pro wrestling autobiographies, which, despite their wildly varying quality, taught me all about the grueling conditions of the business: constant travel and pain, unreliable paychecks, partying, addiction. I've learned that even the best wrestling promoters exploited their workers, and the worst ones were a medley of grifters, thugs, and thieves. Vince McMahon, who I knew then only as the excitable ringside announcer, was the most powerful wrestling promoter in the world, and over the next 30 years he would first become an in-ring performer, and then a close ally of both the Trump administration and the Saudi government, in addition to which he has been frequently accused by employees of horrific sexual misconduct. A disorienting aspect of getting older has been seeing the ways in which public figures from the past never really disappear, they hang around and gradually become worse versions of themselves. It hurts when famous people die because that means you will die too.

As a kid, I had no way of comprehending any of the behind-the-scenes drama. I saw the acrobatics and the flashy costumes and the pure expressions of masculine power, and I loved all of it unconditionally.

It goes without saying that I also had no access to the internal lives of my uncle or my brother at this moment. Every aspect of my experience was superficial.

In 2010, I began working on a novel about pro wrestling, hoping to channel all that youthful enthusiasm and fold in the new insights I had gained. I wrote three-page biographies for all 65 characters who appeared in the book. I drew lines of succession for every title in the history of my fictional wrestling promotion, like I was Marquez detailing the family tree of José Arcadio Buendía. It took me three years to finish a 600-page final draft of *The Three Deaths of Evan Outlaw*, which nobody wanted to publish (after almost a year of submissions, the only note I ever got from an editor was, "It's hard to imagine this as a book"). Despite having published a memoir with a major press, I had still published only two short stories, both for no pay; the book felt like a fluke, and I had convinced myself that this novel would be the one to validate me as a real writer. Because I used to read from the manuscript at events around town and because I talked about it incessantly, people still ask me about the wrestling novel, as if it's ever going to be something besides a large Word document on my computer. Now I tell people it was a valuable learning experience, that I couldn't have written my later work if I hadn't struggled so much with the Evan Outlaw book. This is the kind of comment that sounds true, but I'm not sure if it is. It's at least a more optimistic way of framing having spent three years of my life trying to describe a fisherman suplex in such a way that anybody could ever care.

That book started with someone dying, just like all of my books have. My grad school thesis—an unfinished novel—opened with a murder. The memoir began with my dad's death. The first published novel began with a young wife dying suddenly. The next began with a massacre at a school. I have joked in interviews that my main goal for the next project is to write a book that isn't about people dying. That's why I started this one with a birth. I keep telling people (myself) this one isn't going to be sad.

People who only know me from my writing think I am a dour person, because of how often I come back to death, even in pieces that are not supposed to be about death, as in this instance when I'd love to simply tell you how great the tag team title match between Demolition and The Hart Foundation was, but instead I'm listing body counts. But how am I supposed to talk about anything else here? Your heroes die and if you're lucky they do it before they let you down. I consumed them, all these entertainers, and I gave them nothing in return except this one night of cheering. At the moment, it felt like all I could possibly offer.

1991

Our soccer coach was a man named Jerry who had a mustache like an extra in a Western film, and a thick scar that looked like the laces of a football running down the length of his thigh. His brother Brian helped out sometimes. He had a mustache too, but it was more of a Burt Reynolds, and if he had any scars we couldn't see them. They had both played semi-pro soccer, and their kids were my teammates. They were the first of many coaches I would have over the next 10 years. Later, there would be John, who had the physique of an old-timey circus strongman and jogged for exercise, a hobby that people still viewed with suspicion, if not condescension. Mike, who was just out of college and handsome and therefore the coolest guy we knew, a guy I was convinced would somehow become our friend, a guy whose girlfriend wore cutoff jean shorts and tank tops and when they walked away from practice we all exchanged knowing glances acknowledging that he was a certified sex haver. Luke, a classic biker archetype who one night my friends and I would see drunk by himself sitting on the slide at the playground near my house, and who threatened to stab us if we kept staring at him. Diego, who was from Uruguay and was the most skilled soccer player I would ever meet; he was in his fifties and talked to us too often about our developing testicles, and on more than a few occasions volunteered to drive some of our teammates home after practice, stopping at his house for tea and a nap first (at 12 years old we knew this was weird, but didn't really grasp how weird, or how serious it might be). For the longest stretch, there would be Bradley, a man who seemed to think that having married a Brazil-ian woman had granted him secret soccer knowledge, but he was unable to impart any of it to us. Between scrimmages, he told us stories about running in the mountains of Brazil, as if it had been a religious experience. Over time, he learned to hold us in contempt, and by the time we were old enough to drive ourselves to practice, he showed up late or drunk or both. He lectured us about our defiance and lack of discipline, which often cost us games, but we ignored him because we were teenagers and we wanted to spite him. His son never looked him in the eye. He cried often during games and we ostracized him for his softness. In high school, I would be coached by Kurt, who liked me because I was one of the only city kids on the team. Before practice, we had to find his car in the parking lot and wake him up, because he'd been kicked out of his house; in hindsight, I realize he was living in a perpetual state of being Recently Divorced—nobody in the world has ever been more Recently Divorced than him. On the drive home from one game, he stopped the team van on Roosevelt Boulevard, shifted into park, and made us listen as he sang along to "Lola," which none of us had ever heard before, to his horror. He was a tantrum-throwing coach, the kind who stormed onto the field to grab you and humiliate you in front of everyone for being out of position on a corner kick. At halftime versus North Catholic, he tried to emphasize his anger by kicking over our water jug, and when it didn't spill, he instructed us to pick it up and dump it out because we didn't deserve water. I will never be able to explain why I wanted his approval as badly as I did, but over that summer I called him a few times to let him know I was doing the workouts he'd assigned us. I was tricked into thinking his anger was something like love.

Youth sports are reliant almost entirely on volunteer staff, and kids are at the mercy of which teammates' parents are a) available, b) interested, and c) decent people. If the only parent with an open schedule is a tyrant, then you're stuck, and either you quit the sport or you grow up thinking it's normal for adults to berate children for kicking a ball inaccurately. You learn to make excuses for bullying old men. You say nonsense like, "A coach's job is not to win games, but to mold young men," and so when you find out a coach has been abusing his players, or exploiting their labor for massive profits, or turning a blind eye while an assistant molests them, you already have a lifetime of rationalizations lined up. Unqualified youth sports coaches are the gatekeepers to all kinds of trauma. When you meet an asshole out in the wild, you can safely assume he had an asshole coaching him in baseball when he was nine. Because so many people spend their lives being belittled by authority figures, they learn to believe it's okay for their boss to be like that too. They learn not to value themselves at all. They make excuses for even the worst men. They vote those kinds of men into office because the cruelty is so familiar.

Throughout my youth I will play other sports, but none with the fervor and occasional excitement of soccer. We will win a few city championships, and I will make a few all-star teams. Twenty years later, while cleaning out our basement, my wife will hand me a box of dusty old trophies and say, "What do you want to do with these?" and I will toss them in the trash. There are limits to how much you can carry with you. It all comes down to square footage and how much free time you have.

1992

On a Saturday morning, my Uncle Jim drove me out to another Hamfest, an event where amateur radio enthusiasts gathered in parking lots to trade random assortments of wires and computer chips. Uncle Jim was a career military man who had acquired a serious interest in electronics while in the Navy, and he liked to bring me and Kevin with him when we were free (Kevin was 16 now and worked most Saturdays; his first job was a short-lived stint as a cook at Chili's, but the job I most associate with this period of his life was working the register, and later becoming manager, at CVS, and where he once convinced a co-worker to "catch" me shoplifting on an afternoon when I stopped in with my friends to buy candy. I can admit now that this was a very funny prank for an older brother to have pulled, though at the time I nearly vomited in fear when I felt the co-worker's accusing hand on my shoulder). I didn't comprehend Uncle Jim's electronics demonstrations, and I wasn't much help, but Jim paid me 20 bucks to work at his stand, and 20 bucks was enough to get me to do just about anything when I was 10.

We stopped at McDonald's for breakfast (I don't know how early it was, but I'd felt like we were the only two people alive when he'd picked me up). He ran to the bathroom while I waited for our order. When he came back out, he started laughing—not in a mean way, but in a way that I couldn't quite interpret. I had put a straw in his coffee and he thought this was the funniest thing. He explained that most people don't want to suck streams of boiling hot coffee up through a straw, still laughing. We ate in his van, and I sat in silence while cutting through rubbery pancakes, feeling so stupid, so unworldly, so fundamentally ill-informed that I didn't even know what kind of drinks warranted straws. There is no reason this incident should have affected me the way it did, but I thought about it every day for weeks after. Some mornings, before I was even fully awake, it was the first image to appear in my mind. When I saw my father drinking coffee, I remembered my mistake and wondered how everybody else knew *everything* while I knew *nothing*. There was so much information in the world and I would never even know a fraction of it, and not knowing made me hate myself. This anxiety manifests now in the way I spend all day online, clicking and digging and scrolling, in a futile quest to consume as much content as possible, regardless of its importance or relevance to my life, regardless of how learning it may damage me.

Uncle Jim is a good man who wants to treat people well. A kind man who posts beautiful little notes on Facebook like, "Home some time now, walked out to get the mail. Realize someone had plowed my driveway. Have no idea who," and "Made progress on clearing my yard today. My 73-year-old knees slowed my 30-year-old body down. Takes more effort to move on the knees so I had to rest a lot more than I like. Still I made progress." He lives in rural New Jersey now, about an hour from me, and although he's been retired from the military for a long time, he stays busier and more active than most people half his age. Lately, he's been building solar-powered car batteries, just to see if he can; when he explains how they work, I don't understand any of it, though Kevin, now an engineer, is able to follow along. Sometimes Kevin tries to translate it for me, and I trust him that it all makes sense.

He still used the straw I gave him with his coffee, even though he obviously didn't really want to. People drink coffee through straws all the time now. Everything we know about coffee is different today; it's barely the same product. Ten-year-olds have coffee every morning. They carry it into school with them like stern old men on their way to a board meeting.

38

While we ate, I tried to distract myself by listening to the lyrics of the songs on the oldies station, and I realized, suddenly, that "Under the Boardwalk" is about sex. I was unprepared in every way for this breakthrough, for seeing my uncle drumming his fingers on the steering wheel as Johnny Moore sang that he and his baby would be makin' love, for recalling my own mom having sung along with the same lyrics with gusto. It would be an exaggeration to call this the end of my innocence, but it did feel like I'd stepped out of one world and into another. I wondered how many other songs were about sex. I began to suspect that everything I could see was a pleasant façade hiding something much weirder and more dangerous. I worry now that I'm over-intellectualizing this story, twisting a couple simple moments into something much bigger than they were. But how else does one explain these two otherwise trivial incidents sticking in my memory for 30 years?

There are important ways in which my default skepticism protects me still. The world gives us very little reason to believe that good things will stay good. Writers I admire are revealed to be sex pests. Institutions I once believed in turn out to be predatory and criminal. Neighbors go to jail for crimes you never thought possible. The government devolves further into a playground for a handful of billionaires to practice social engineering.

This cynicism is surely what's going to kill me. If I could turn it off, I think I would. Ignorance isn't truly bliss, but it's something better than this.

I bought three computer games at the Hamfest, stacks of 3.5-inch floppy disks that I patiently fed to the computer for an hour that evening. One was *Wolfenstein 3D*, one of the pioneers in the first-person shooter genre, in which you navigate the halls of various Nazi facilities and shoot German soldiers as they shout *Achtung!* It was a simple time. We all agreed that Nazis were bad then. All summer, I shot Nazi after Nazi. I shot so many Nazis, you wouldn't believe it. I dreamed about killing them. I was very good at video games during this time. I bet I could still pile up bodies if you set me up right now. Maybe that doesn't matter, but it felt like a real achievement then. You have to take the victories where you can get them.

1993

The cool kids in sixth grade had haircuts we called mushrooms: a fade stuck in a bad marriage with a bowl cut. I wanted the same haircut as those guys because girls talked to them and I also wanted to be talked to by girls. My dad took me to Tom & Al's, a local institution where everyone knew that Al gave good haircuts and Tom did not, a fact I took personally, as if somehow I was accountable for the performance of all Toms everywhere (one of our regular games at recess was listing famous people with our names, and so I had compiled a thorough inventory of all known Toms, both good and bad). People sometimes waited an hour for Al, while Tom sat in his chair reading *Playboy*. I tried not to be caught peeking at the *Playboy*. The men around me talked about sports and women and how young people were not as good as they used to be. When a Dr. Dre song came on the radio, one man demanded that Tom turn off the "jungle music."

I have never in my life had cool hair. The year before, I had mimicked Kevin's hairstyle and gotten a flattop, a boxy, weird haircut that held its shape when brushed back with a glue stick-like product called Stix Fix. The best-case scenario was to look like Brian Bosworth, and the worst was to look like you had just failed the police exam for the third time. One of the older kids on the bus told me my head looked like a whitewall tire, an insult that made no sense to me then or now, but nonetheless upset me enough that a few days after this, I punched that guy's younger brother in the back. Later, as a college freshman, I tried to grow my hair out like Jim Morrison's, but it kept getting thicker and hotter and frizzier (on Instant Messenger, I told a girl I liked that I was growing it out, and the next time she saw me she said, "You look exactly the same"). Now, as more of my forehead reveals itself each year, my main goal is to try not to look disheveled or too old.

My dad didn't want to wait for Al, so he made me go to Tom. I was too shy to specifically request a mushroom, so I got a blocky and uneven fade instead. I wore a hat every day to hide it—a *Pinky and the Brain* ballcap my grandmother had bought me. While waiting for the bus, a classmate named Alissa turned to me and asked: "Why do you wear your hat so low?" We rarely spoke to each other, but I'd had a crush on her for as long as I was aware of the possibility of having crushes. I told her I was wearing it that way as a joke, and to prove I didn't care about my hat at all, I ripped it off and threw it into the bushes and decided never again to wear a hat. There is no way she remembers this conversation. She may not even remember me.

Everything changed, hairwise, in our school when Nick, one of the cool kids showed up with his head shaved. The day before, he and his younger brother had had their bikes stolen by "some kids from Shawmont," which was one of the public schools nearby, and which we all understood to mean "some Black kids." There are racists everywhere, but I didn't realize until I'd lived outside this area how differently it manifests by location; in Philly, it is open and aggressive, whereas in other parts of the country, it's more subdued and polite, though just as destructive. In grad school, I included the detail about "jungle music" in a short story, and a classmate who had grown up richer than anyone I have ever met said, "I don't understand—is this story set in, like, the fifties?" Casual racism was part of the atmosphere. Groups of men sat in circles and unhinged their jaws and let all the world's garbage spew out onto the floor, and then they invited the kids to play in it.

Nick's father, a Philly cop, was enraged, not at the thieves, but at his sons for having been robbed. He whipped his kids with a belt and then sat them in kitchen chairs and shaved their heads. They both had abrasions on their skulls where he'd shaved too aggressively. He told them, "If you didn't have those ni---- haircuts you wouldn't have got robbed," which was presented to us as a punchline. Because you could still get detention for using that word at school, many guys had turned it around and called each other "Reggin" as a way of sneaking the slur into daily conversation. A guy named Eric had learned this trick from his father, also a cop. This was back when everyone's mom was a nurse and everyone else's dad was a cop (my dad did every other possible job at some point: door-to-door sales, mail delivery, restaurants, truck driving, warehouses, computers). I never used the word myself, but I stood there and laughed when everyone else said it, so who cares about me? I laughed at every racist joke, especially the ones I didn't really comprehend. I was a coward then and I'm often a coward now.

In my first book, I told the story of attending a neighborhood Christmas party in my first year as a homeowner in the Jersey suburbs, standing among a group of men and feeling that change in the atmosphere when one of the guys looked over his shoulder and realized *we're all white here* and nobody could yell at him for what he was about to say. He leaned in like a child on the playground telling a joke he'd stolen from his drunk uncle, some gag about monkeys or Obama or African names. Another guy bragged about the tricks he'd used to deter a Black family from buying the house where we now lived. Later, one of these guys pointed at my Honda Civic and asked why I was driving "a Dink car," a slur I had never even heard before. When I saw one of those neighbors reading my book on his porch, I rushed across the street to reassure him that story was actually about racists in my old neighborhood. "I would hate to think we lived near anyone who thought like that," he said. But it was him who had made the jokes. He was the racist in the book, and he didn't even remember it, or he did and he was daring me to call his bluff.

I am trying to get better at interrupting, saying, "I don't really like this conversation," or "I think you've got this all wrong," or *something.* It's not enough to just not be racist, or to feel bad about it; silence is a tacit approval of everyone else's racist bullshit. A whole life devoted to avoiding awkwardness is pointless.

Well-meaning people have always pushed the notion that we just have to wait out the racists and watch them die off. The past few years have been a stark reminder of how stupid this idea is, how shortsighted and meaningless, to think the only way to fight racism is to hang around and wait a while. Thanks to Facebook, I know Nick and his brother are Trump supporters and they spend days posting cruel memes about lazy Mexicans and Black thugs. They love the concept of walls, generally, and feel that most liberals should probably be put in jail, just to be safe. One of them has kids and they'll grow up the same way. It all keeps going.

After Nick and his brother got their heads shaved, everyone else followed. The principal sent a note home to parents addressing concerns that the head shaving was somehow a gang symbol. My mom took me to get my head shaved too. In the middle of the shave, Tom stopped and called her over to say, "Something's wrong here," one of the worst statements you can hear from any barber. My head was covered in scaly, peeling skin. Because I was half-shaved the only option was to finish the job and figure out the rest later. Within the space of our two-mile drive home, I convinced myself it was a terminal illness. It all scrubbed off in the shower, which meant it was probably just shampoo I had rubbed into my head without adequately rinsing. I spent the night lying in bed and wishing my hair could grow back, vowing never to cut it again. But hair grows at whatever rate it feels like growing. All I wanted then was to fundamentally change myself, but nothing I tried worked. I was changing all the time, but it was all out of my control.

1994

For as many hours per day as I was allowed to be online, I posted in the Prodigy forums for sports, music, and "teen interests," and I came to view two other regular posters as nemeses. They didn't know they were my enemies until the day I was banned from the forums. One posted mostly about heavy metal and idolized Trent Reznor, even changing his display name from Dan to Trent in homage. I envied him because he was a few years older than me and he'd boasted about having girlfriends and said he listened to Nine Inch Nails while having sex. I was at the age when I believed anything an older kid said about sex, even if they referred to it as "bumping n' grinding."

There are several people on Facebook now with his name, but only one who wears leather jackets and has shoulder-length hair and is sharing Nine Inch Nails and System of a Down music videos. In the most recent photos, his weird goatee makes him look like a guy who would do magic on the street. He has a full sleeve of tattoos and is working on a second one. He enjoys drinking Yuengling with his buddies and holding guitars in various garages and basements. He appears to have done some musical theater in high school.

I spent almost an hour scouring his page before registering that his name was followed by "Jr." I had wanted it to be my old Prodigy enemy because I felt a strange connection to this guy, the first I'd ever fought with online. But he's too young. The *West Side Story* pictures aren't throwback images; they're from when he was in high school in 2009. This kid is young enough that he could be my son. There is only one picture of him with his parents, who appear to be in their early forties. His mom looks like she grew up on the South Jersey shore and used to wear toe rings and sit on the lawn at Red Hot Chili Peppers concerts, drinking Gatorade spiked with vodka. Dan Sr. looks like a guy who owns a stucco company, and who complains about how the new cell phones are too confusing. If this is the guy I knew in the 1990s, I bet he keeps an iPod loaded with NIN songs in his car, and on nice days he rolls the windows down and bangs his head to "March of the Pigs" and tries to transport himself back to those teen years when anything seemed possible. I thought about sending Dan Jr. a message to ask if his dad remembers Prodigy. If he remembers his login info (my username was MEBD92D, a sequence that flows automatically from my fingers). It might not even be him in the picture, but I want it to be him.

My other enemy was named Pete and his last name is unusual enough that he is easy to find. He's in his late thirties and runs a podcast consulting business—which I now know is a job a person can have—in addition to a variety of side hustles that all fold into something that might be labeled: *life coach* or *thinkfluencer*. That he hasn't done a TEDx talk yet is the most shocking detail I've learned about him. His online presence is relentlessly cheery and he writes posts like, "You need a clear and actionable road map to achieve your goals." He promises to, "Enhance your thinking" and help you cut every wasted minute from your day. You will, "Find your inner power" following his patented steps. He brags that his, "Work has enriched many *Fortune* 100 companies," which I am aware is a thing some people value.

I am skeptical of all people in this weird field of non-work, this zone that exists between people with jobs and the people who want to fire those people. It's like being a self-appointed hall monitor. Any system that reduces people to their productivity hours is a diseased system. Fuck maximizing your productivity hours. The whole industry of making people feel guilty for not doing enough work is nauseating. It kills people and then tells them it's their fault for dying, and then sends a bill.

46

It's not fair for me to dislike Pete now. He may have helped a lot of people. He may be a good citizen and family member. He's trying to survive, and he found that he's good at this job I neither understand nor respect. I despised him 30 years ago because he was constantly needling me, undermining my comments, pointing out typos and grammar errors. He crossed the line when he called me a "poseur," which at the time was the greatest insult I knew. He said I was pretending to like Metallica to fit in. Dan/Trent chimed in to agree. So I had my first-ever online meltdown.

The subject was "Peter [REDACTED]!!!" and the message was over 500 words long. I used the word "pussy" (spelled like this: Pu$$y) several times. I told him I would murder him if we ever met. I posted it before I went to bed, and overnight my dad got an email saying I'd been banned. He printed my post and highlighted every profanity. He wanted me to know my mom was disappointed to see me using this language. At times like this, I wished I had a dad who would yell at me instead of asking me to explain the stupid things I'd done. He had an explosive temper, which we saw occasionally, but now I think his insistence on talking out problems was primarily driven by fear of losing control of his own anger. I believe it because I do the same.

Because my dad had a longstanding interest in computers, we were early adopters of most technologies, so I was banned from an online message board before most people in the world had ever logged on. I feel like being a veteran of these battles gives me some kind of credibility, but I'm not sure what to do with it. Much of my subsequent life would be spent engaged in new fights in various online forums, from AOL chat rooms to private message boards to all manner of social media. I rarely fight online anymore, but it took 25 years of wasted energy to get here. Still, I devote an inordinate amount of time to learning more about each new awful person the internet presents to me, even if it's some guy on Twitter with eight followers and a tenuous grasp on how to write a sentence. I'll spend an hour reading through all of his tweets. I'll screenshot the worst ones and save them, just in case. Exposing myself to the dumbest ideas and the most hateful weirdos online triggers a chemical reaction that gives me pleasure, or something like it.

Around the same time as my Prodigy ban, I had cultivated an intense real-life grudge against the other Tom in my class, who was more popular and more athletic and richer. He had a treehouse with a zipline that ran to the other end of the yard. In fifth grade he had won a spelling bee in which I'd been eliminated early after panicking on an easy word. He never did anything specifically to hurt me, but I viewed each of his successes as an insult.

When I won a limo ride through a school raffle (I'd sold seven magazine subscriptions in one of those bizarre fundraisers that turn kids into door-to-door salesmen), I invited him instead of my best friend to be my plus-one, a popularity power play. The theory was: I give him the limo ride, he decides I'm cool, and then there is a declaration of my coolness to everyone else. Just by existing as a popular person, you get free gifts handed to you. We were supposed to drive past our homes, flaunt our fanciness, and then get lunch from McDonald's while our classmates stayed behind, learning about gerunds and envying us. The limo couldn't get down my narrow street safely, so we drove past a nearby intersection and honked the horn. Tom's road was wide enough, his house big enough, that we crawled past while his mom stood outside and waved. My McDonald's order was all wrong—I wanted a plain cheeseburger, but I got the sauce and the pickles and everything—so I took one bite of my burger and threw out my fries out of spite. I never became popular, and I blamed all of this on Tom. These days, he works as a producer on a TV show for a particularly odious Fox News personality, which is to say: I might have disliked him unfairly, but I wasn't wrong. Most of my enemies have never known they're my enemies, but that doesn't make the fights we've had any less real.

48

1995

Near the end of seventh grade, we had to complete a Sacraments of Initiation Booklet, writing brief narratives about each of the sacraments we had received, tracing our personal transformation thanks to having been filled with God's grace. For each sacrament, I focused my story on the fact that we went out to celebrate afterward at D'Angelo's Summit, the only nice restaurant in the neighborhood. On the final page, under the heading *Future Me*, I write:

"I hope to be a good, caring person. I hope to be a professional athlete in the future, but if I do not succeed in that, I want to work with animals. In the future, I could give money to the parish, put money in the poor box, and help take care of my parents."

Under the heading *Hospitality, Service, and Me*, I write:

"When I'm with my friends, I help them if they are hurt and I am nice to them. In my parish, I try to help the people around me and help old people carry things."

That second sentence is arguably the funniest line I've ever written. I imagine seventh grade me chasing down old people and demanding that they allow me to carry their things. Old people throughout the city, helpless and laden with bowling balls and lug wrenches and other burdens that can only be carried by me. Me going door to door with an empty sack and asking local old people to fill it up with all their wishes and regrets. One can only hope that some young person has stepped up to fill the void since I left town.

Even taking into account that I was at this point deeply distrustful of the institution of the Church, this is a surprisingly lazy effort. I am disappointed in the shallowness of my thought, the sloppiness of my prose. I feel guilty about the time my teacher had to waste reading this. I don't know what grade I received, though I obsessed over such things then, even when I didn't care about the content of the work. It wasn't until much later that I learned your grades have no bearing on your life outside of school.

The booklet is, infuriatingly, not organized chronologically, and so the first page features a picture of me in my Confirmation garb, standing alongside my grandmother, who was my sponsor. She'd cried when I asked her to be my sponsor, a decision I did not consider seriously, because I did not take the sacrament itself seriously. My Confirmation name was Damien, which I had chosen because my friends and I thought it was funny. I never understood what I was supposed to get out of Jesus. I smuggled *Far Side* books into church with me, and once a nun caught me and announced to my entire class that I deserved the Sneak of the Year Award.

When I talk about Catholic schooling, non-Catholics usually make some comment about the priests, a joke about molestation. For some reason, this is a joke people still think is funny. Two of our best-liked priests ended up on the lists of abusers in the Diocese. Both were reassigned to new parishes. In Camden County, New Jersey, where I live now, the Diocese recently released a list of 56 more priests who have been identified as serial abusers, though they waited until most of these men were dead to share their names. One of these priests gave a moving sermon at my father-in-law's funeral, and afterward we all raved about how he was the kind of priest we wished we'd had when we were growing up. The likelihood is that I do know someone who has been abused by priests. It's a great ongoing crime against humanity, reduced too often to a naughty little joke. I have been to Catholic churches a few times since leaving high school, but only for weddings and funerals. I try to be polite to my host. I go through the motions. I often find myself mouthing responses out of habit. The hymns are still inside of me, whether I want them there or not.

My grandmother had devoted most of her life to serving the Church in one way or another. In retirement, she volunteered at the St. John the Baptist rectory, doing odd jobs: cooking, stuffing mailers, answering the phone, proofreading the bulletin. She delivered care packages to ill and disabled parishioners, and she was in charge of ferrying a statue of the Virgin Mary between homes across the city. It was the size of a bedside lamp, and heavy enough that I needed both hands to carry it. It migrated to a new home each week, promising comfort and healing to good Catholics praying for miracles. I was there for many of these deliveries because my grandmother was my primary caretaker while my parents were at work. I'm sure she hoped to impress upon me the importance of helping people in specific, meaningful ways.

We entered one woman's house—I think her name was Helen, but for a brief period I believed every woman over 60 was named Helen—and found her on the floor in the back bedroom. Helen was clearly alive and yet the stale odor of the house, the helplessness of her sitting upright on the floor with her hands in her lap, the eerie chill in the air made it feel like we had stumbled into a crypt. My grandmother, exasperated, shouted: "You know you're not supposed to be on the floor!"

Helen: "I saw lint on the rug and couldn't stand looking at it."

My grandmother's heavy sigh. Calling me to help her lift this woman off the floor and guide her back to the couch.

She was an actual good person, my grandmother, the kind who I have to remind myself are everywhere, and though she was working on behalf of a rotten institution, the positive impact she made was real and tangible. I didn't appreciate how good she was until long after her death, which occurred within a year of my Confirmation. My mom's mother would die soon after. I didn't comprehend until much later what a profound loss this was for my mom, with her father already dead for so long. She told me once about seeing her mother's body in the hospital and trying to convince her sisters not to come in and look at it. I had no idea they were fighting with each other at the time—years of conflicts coming to a head in the arguments over what to do with their childhood home—but I was at an age where adult problems weren't interesting to me. My mom's mother has a burial plot near the edge of the cemetery, and she always told her daughters, "You don't even have to get out of the car, just drive by and toss some flowers from the window." Now my mom says the same to us about the plot she'll one day share with my dad.

I went to my grandmothers' funerals with no understanding of how one is supposed to act, and I read the pamphlets they gave me at the funeral home. My dad asked me how I felt and I shrugged and he asked again and I shrugged again and he asked if I was fine and I said I was fine.

A week later, my mom got a call from the school because I'd been in a fight at recess. This was nothing new; we all got in fights, all the time. Fighting got you attention. It was a preemptive strike to signal that you couldn't be bullied. It felt good, to get hit and hit back. A bruise or a black eye gave you something to fixate on when you were alone. My mom told the principal both my grandmothers had died and I was having a hard time with it, and so I didn't get any punishment. The kid I'd fought got suspended for a week, and last I checked he's in jail, though it would be hard to draw a straight line between those facts.

My dad wrote a letter to me to end the sacraments booklet. It's the only sincere effort in there. He stresses the importance of loving Jesus, and he ends like this:

"Please remember that hate is a negative emotion, and you cannot hate someone and love Christ. You can hate their actions, but you should not hate them. The emotion of hate detracts from you as a person and makes it more difficult to show your love of Jesus."

I don't know much about Jesus, but I know about hate, and I know when I was 13 I rolled my eyes at that letter, and I never envisioned this version of me, 29 years later, fatherless for most of them, finding it and trying not to cry in front of my wife, trying to turn it into a joke, somehow.

1996

In eighth grade, we read *Catcher in the Rye* and *Of Mice and Men*; I spent the next two years imitating Salinger and Steinbeck. Every short story I wrote opened with lush descriptions of valleys and rivers, phenomena I didn't care about and had only occasionally observed. My protagonists were obsessed with suicide. Every story included a beautiful woman named Alexa, inspired by Alissa, the girl I thought I loved even though we barely spoke to each other (my friends had once convinced me to call her and ask her on a date; when she answered, I said, "I know you from school," a line from *The Simpsons*, and then I hung up, an even less effective approach than it sounds). One of my favorite stories ended with a giant Pac-Man eating a lion before the lion could eat Alexa. Good ideas are good ideas.

Kevin, who had read *Catcher in the Rye* in high school (he was in college by this point, but lived close enough that he was home regularly), helped me to understand some of the book's symbolism, so in my essay I wrote about the brass ring and innocence and all that kind of crap. My teacher held me after class and said I shouldn't let my parents do my work for me. She couldn't prove I'd cheated, or that my parents were the types to write a paper for me, so I wouldn't get punished as long as I turned in a new essay. I spent the next few days intentionally writing a worse paper to avoid exceeding the low expectations of my teacher.

Later that year, I read a Heinlein novel about a futuristic, waterless society, and instead of writing a traditional book report, I spent days mocking up a four-page newspaper from this fictional world. Our temperamental dot-matrix printer continually jammed and chewed up my pages, while I cursed and begged it to cooperate with my vision. I did not get an A on the assignment because I hadn't followed directions. When they asked us to write poetry, I turned in something cynical and dark about corrupt police (I didn't know anything about police corruption, but I knew it as a concept), and the principal called my parents in for a meeting. "We'd rather he just write something nice," he said.

In Catholic school, my job was to show up and shut up and fill in the blanks. The whole point is to be mediocre enough not to draw attention to yourself. Failing meant you were especially bad. Excelling meant you were still bad, but in a different way. When I teach college freshmen now, I can tell the students who have come to me from 12 years of Catholic school because they may be polite and quiet, but they also have no idea how to join a conversation. They are uncomfortable with open-ended assignments. They want to be told exactly how to write each sentence. If they'd ever tried to challenge themselves, their teachers shut it down as quickly as possible. I'm lucky to have inherited my parents' stubbornness.

Our eighth-grade teachers always told us we were the worst group they'd ever had. A student two years before us had poisoned a teacher's Diet Coke with dog shampoo, and another had been arrested for selling drugs on school grounds, so this always struck me as a little overblown. Probably it was something they said to every group, a pedagogy based on shame. They held a big ceremony at the start of the year to unveil the school's new slogan—FRO, or *Faith, Respect, Obedience.* Our pastor stood on stage, defining each word, detailing the ways in which we were lacking. While he spoke, someone blurted out a high-pitched squeal, our cohort's understanding of what a woman sounded like during sex. The principal picked up the handbell that usually signaled the end of recess, and he stomped around the room ringing it in people's faces. "That person. The one who made that sound," he said, still ringing, "Will come to me now."

Nobody came to him. We already understood that he wielded no real power. Our school had divested itself of the nuns and other trappings of the Catholic schooling our parents, and even my brother, had known: the cruel, petty, tyranny of rulers cracked against knuckles, the paralyzing fear of the church's authority figures. What remained was a husk of the past, a nostalgia for a time when teachers could hit the students and get away with it. The principal rang the bell again and we went back to our classrooms where we memorized the Beatitudes. It's hard to overemphasize how pointless it all was.

One afternoon six of us got in trouble for having in some way demonstrated inadequate levels of F, R, or O. We were removed from the classroom and sat on the floor of the principal's office— he had chairs, but our chair privileges had been revoked. For the rest of the day, we wrote on scratch paper, "I will show the proper respect and obedience to my school and Jesus Christ." In the middle I mixed in my own sentences, sneaking in curse words and inside jokes. Nobody would ever read any of it. When the principal left us alone in his office, we rifled through his drawers looking for something embarrassing or incriminating, but all we found were files. He was the biggest villain in our world, but he was, I now realize, just a middle-aged guy doing a job he hated. That evening, my dad wrote a letter to the principal saying he understood I deserved to be disciplined but wished it could be done in a meaningful way that didn't remove me from class. The next day, the principal read the note, shook his head, and threw it out without saying anything. What else is there to say about school? No wonder so many kids are ruined for education by the time they get to my classroom. No wonder so many people think it's all a waste of time.

1997

A couple years after my grandmother's death, my Uncle Mike fell behind on tax payments and the bank repossessed the house he had inherited from her, the same house in which he'd been raised with my dad and their sister. I knew nothing about his life then; though he took us to occasional Phillies games and once to SummerSlam, I could go months without talking to him. He smoked constantly and had speckled the couch with little burn holes by falling asleep with lit cigarettes in his mouth. He owned a signed Steve Jeltz home run ball and a fist-sized piece of the Berlin Wall, which sat side-by-side on top of a bookshelf. In old photo albums there are pictures of him at one of my birthday parties with a black eye; I later was told that he'd been attacked outside a bar the night before because he was gay (I can't say anything for sure about his sexual orientation, but this is the commonly accepted explanation in my family). I didn't know until much later that he'd struggled with drug and alcohol addiction. He's still alive and on Facebook—he's been sober a while and works for a church in North Philly—but we haven't spoken since my dad's funeral 21 years ago. I never had a sense of how my dad felt about his own brother, besides being frustrated with him. He'd waited too long to ask for help, and now we had one weekend to clear out a three-story home that had been overstuffed with five decades worth of clutter.

I have never worked harder in my life, nor for so little reward. We put in 14-hour days, hauling bag after bag after bag of trash to the local landfill. The dump was open to the public then. You could drive in and drop your trash in the pile, no questions asked. There was a time when you could throw your garbage directly into the incinerator, until the city realized it might be hazardous to have thousands of pounds of toxic ash festering in the middle of our neighborhood. I learned more about the ash pile years later, when I was digging through *Philadelphia Inquirer* archives for an unrelated project. That ash spent more than a decade on a barge called *The Khian Sea* until finally it was illegally dumped in Haiti. Incinerated scraps of cloth, boxes of books, thousands of empty beer bottles, splintered drawers and end tables. Whatever it used to be, it was all just garbage. Still, nobody will take responsibility for it. Eventually, even our trash colonizes the developing world.

Between this grueling weekend and LauraBeth's own experiences sorting through the detritus of her deceased parents' lives, we both have developed an intense aversion to surrounding ourselves with clutter and leaving it for others to collect and categorize and throw into dumpsters. Once a year we work through our house and eliminate all the excess junk, and despite our vigilance, we still have 10 bags of trash to haul to the curb and two carloads of odds and ends to deliver to Goodwill. I don't know where it all comes from, the junk. It reproduces on its own and tries to fill every square foot of your home. We manage it with baskets and shelves and in-drawer organizers, and when they overflow, we go to The Container Store for contraptions to hold our baskets. Half of what we donate ends up in a dumpster before anyone has a chance to buy it, and somehow it all ends up adhering to the garbage island in the Pacific Ocean. Eventually, your things find their way back to their own kind, clumping and floating like the eighth continent, this grim new ecosystem of plastic bottles and knickknacks and other objects that used to be treasured by people who were alive.

My dad showed me the room where his sister Molly used to sleep. She'd had a seizure one night when she was 30 and died in her bed. I had only met her as a baby, but I heard about her often enough to know her premature death had scarred everyone in that family in ways I will never fully fathom. Kevin has some memories of her; given our age difference, he has access to a trove of family stories that are all abstractions to me. My dad very rarely spoke about his sister, and when my Uncle Mike did, he struggled not to cry. When their mother was getting older, she sometimes called my mom Molly, and nobody corrected her because it was obviously a term of endearment. Most of her belongings were still in the same place as the day she died. We dumped the contents of her drawers into trash bags and then we dragged the furniture down a winding staircase and then dropped it on the curb for a junk man to find.

My uncle had two friends helping, younger Black men I'd never met before. One wore a t-shirt stylized to look like a Wheaties box, except it said WEEDIES and had an image of a Rasta man smoking a joint on the front. The other owned a dog named Satan. Later, my uncle would have a falling out with Satan's owner; without any evidence, I had always assumed it was somehow about gambling debts. Uncle Mike would describe this man and Satan as his enemies and tell me not to trust anything they said. I couldn't imagine a scenario where I would run into Satan or his owner. This isn't metaphor. It was just a dog's name.

When I was older, my mom would strongly imply that the man in the WEEDIES shirt was my uncle's boyfriend. Until the end of high school, I had never knowingly associated with a gay person, and I had no understanding then of the difficulty of growing up closeted in a devoutly Catholic household. On top of that, dating a Black man in our racist little neighborhood—it was beyond my comprehension, beyond my effort.

Recently, my uncle sent me a direct message on Facebook. It had been sitting there a couple weeks before I noticed. It began, "I just read your book," meaning my memoir. In that book, I describe him as a drunk and a loser, unreliable and dishonest and self-destructive; his role in the book is to be a contrast to my deceased father, and also to process my own worries about being the Bad Brother in contrast to Kevin's Good Brother. I don't know if I was being unfair to him. I was so angry still, about everything. His note was a long one, long enough I had to scroll down to skim to the end. I saw numerous words in caps (NEVER and NO ONE and I DIDN'T and YOU LIED), which was enough for me to get the gist. He felt betrayed. I did betray him in the sense that I never tried to know him. At the end of my dad's funeral, he asked for the printed copy of my eulogy; I wonder if it's still in his possession. I wonder if he tells his church group about his cold-hearted and ungrateful nephew. When he dies, I won't know about it for weeks.

By the end of that weekend, we had emptied the house, and only when we sat on the front stoop eating cheesesteaks—the most satisfying meal of my life, considering my exhaustion—did I realize how sad my dad was. He clapped his hand on my shoulder and told me he loved me—not unusual for him, but for a brief moment, I felt his full weight on me, as if I was the only thing keeping him on his feet. The house he'd grown up in was gone. His brother was never going to become the person my dad wished he could be. I was 15 and convinced that I understood the world better than anyone. I've tried to bury that arrogant, narrow-minded version of me, but some days I want to resurrect him. I want to cling to that defiance, and that confidence. It never felt good, exactly, but it felt like a direction.

1998

My mom would eventually tell me about sitting outside the bathroom door listening for the sound of vomiting. I lost 50 pounds during sophomore year and she was convinced I was bulimic. This was the first time in my life that I had exercised seriously. I had been cut from the JV soccer team, but the coach asked me to stay on as the manager, which meant I got to do all the running and practicing without actually getting to play in the games. I had never liked my body before, and I have rarely liked it since, but suddenly it could do things I never thought possible. I was in better shape than everyone on the team. I once ran two miles in 10:20, and that was after a two-hour practice. Even still, there was no activity that filled me with more dread than running, and for years the smell of freshly cut grass would make me vaguely nauseous. I was having no fun playing soccer, but I got to throw out my size-40 pants. I got to take my shirt off on the beach. I got to see myself in the mirror and think: *Someone could like this.*

Every day I logged on to AOL and typed *Keyword: Acne*, hoping for a new magic solution. I had already tried 17 treatments, a mix of prescription antibiotics, over-the-counter stuff, and home remedies. One face wash was so harsh that over time most of my shirts would be freckled with bleach stains around the collars. The dermatologist wanted to prescribe Accutane, a miracle drug that was accompanied by a vast list of severe side effects, including suicidal depression. I told the doctor I was afraid of what I would do to myself. I was sad then and sometimes thought it would be glamorous to be sadder than I was. I had recently told my school counselor I'd experienced suicidal thoughts, but that wasn't true; I'd only considered the possibility of having suicidal thoughts. I didn't want to risk my life over vanity, I said. My mom said I'd made a mature choice, but most days I regretted it, and kept doing the math, trying to calculate precisely how depressed I was willing to feel in exchange for a normal face.

I flew to Atlanta with my parents for a family wedding. I wasn't invited but they didn't want to leave me home alone. We went to the Coca-Cola Factory and the zoo and the Underground and I don't remember what else. The night of the wedding, I sat in the hotel room by myself watching *Good Will Hunting* on pay-per-view. I ordered a large Domino's pizza and bought a six-pack of Yoo-hoo bottles and consumed all of it, thinking: *This is what it means to be an adult. Nobody can stop you.* In the future you can go wherever you want and if you want pizza then you just get pizza. I still get excited to check in to a hotel room, some lingering memory of this night when I felt oddly free. At that age, with vague aspirations of one day being a writer, the movie itself struck me as *important*. The story of two youngish pals from Boston writing a movie together launched me into daydreams of doing the same with my friends. It didn't seem very difficult. You come up with an idea for a movie, then you write the movie. Why couldn't we do that?

Driving courses at AAA required 30 classroom hours, during which we spent a quarter of our time watching videos about how dangerous trucks are, including a rap video about the importance of avoiding the "no zones;" during which I sat next to someone with a developmental disability, who was mocked relentlessly by two guys I was sure were the cool kids at their high school; during which I noticed the cool kids had begun sitting on either side of me so they could copy my answers on the tests, and I started intentionally writing wrong answers so they would get poor grades, my own sad vigilante justice; during which I met Diane, who would one day take me to her senior prom, and who would eventually become one of the very few people from this time who I still consider a friend; during which we milled around outside on our lunch break and saw a desperate man sprint past us and disappear into the thin line of trees at the edge of the parking lot, followed seconds later by three police officers shouting at us to get back inside, an incident that was never explained; during which, forced to take my 10 hours of on-road instruction, I drove 15 miles per hour along the shoulder of Germantown Pike until the instructor took over for me; during which I had to admit to my dad that I was sure I would die the first time I drove alone, and, instead of being disappointed in me, he told me it's okay to be afraid but we can't let fear dictate all of our choices; during which all I could see were worst-case scenarios no matter what else was happening, visions of trucks decapitating me or overturning and crushing me or even exploding while I tried to pass, in a rush to get to nowhere specific.

I was standing outside with Joe, a neighbor a year younger than me, who had grown up in the kind of home where they have to open the windows periodically to let all the screams out. I was on scholarship at a suburban prep school and he was failing out of the school up the road that was then on Philly's list of "chronically dangerous" high schools. His future was bad and mine was not, and our future selves stood there between us, hating each other. Maybe that's why, as I strolled a few feet away from him, he picked up a tennis ball-sized rock and threw it directly at the side of my head. After it hit me, I charged and punched him twice, before an adult leaned out a window to yell at us. I walked back toward my house and he followed, taunting me. "Look at this bitch," he said. "Gets mad when you throw rocks at him. Like a bitch." Who wouldn't get mad about someone throwing rocks at them? How was that even an insult?

On Christmas Eve, I was in my Aunt Judy's kitchen waving a towel to waft smoke out the window as they fried up another batch of pierogis (the smoke is normal, the sizzling of several pounds of butter is normal). The door opened and my Aunt Diane and her husband Lance entered, followed by their son, Lance. Young Lance was in his mid-twenties and weighed over 500 pounds. He tripped

63

through the doorway and fell into the room. The impact of a man his size rattled the dishes on the table. He was helpless and embarrassed; Kevin and my dad rushed to help him up. Witnessing what I assumed to be one of the worst moments of Lance's life, I was too afraid to join them, and wished I could disappear. He was a jovial and gregarious guy, and when they got him to his feet, he made a joke and people started talking again, but I never forgot the image of him, half inside and half out, his shirt having ridden up, his body so large and so damaged. He would be dead within a year. That night, I ate and I ate and I ate. I made sure my mouth was always full, focused exclusively on chewing, swallowing, digesting.

One of the few rituals we maintain in our family is the Polish tradition of the oplatek—just before Christmas Eve dinner, my mom distributes graham cracker-sized wafers embossed with Christian imagery, flavorless and a little stale. Everyone gets their own and has to work the room snapping a piece off the others' oplatek, and wishing them health, wealth, and happiness. By the end, you have eaten chunks of everyone else's wafers and have given away all of yours, sharing a moment of communal goodwill before the main course. When I was 16, I misunderstood the purpose of the ritual, and I thought these three resources—health, wealth, happiness— were finite, so that if I had all three, then Lance could have none, and if I wished them too sincerely for someone else, I would lose them all. None of it is permanent, and the whole point is that you should do whatever you can to share it with others. When you're young you want wealth and when you're old you want health and in the middle you convince yourself that what you deserve is happiness, even if it's not what you have. You have to figure out how to make it all work in the meantime.

1999

This was the year everyone paired off with serious girlfriends. It was the year we all started to harbor intense resentments of those girl-friends—never of our friends themselves, always the girls—because they were interrupting our routines and insisting on being included. The greatest offense one could commit at that time was to go out alone with his girlfriend leaving us to do the same old activities (going to the movies, meandering from one end of the mall to the other and back, playing video games), except with one less guy. The second greatest offense was to invite the girlfriend to join us. We became experts in cataloguing every imperfection, any flaw we could observe or invent. We muttered and laughed at inside jokes in front of the girlfriends, too gutless to confront them, but cruel enough to let them know they weren't welcome. We used the term "whipped" constantly and made whipping sounds at one another. We solemnly repeated mantras like "Bros before hos" if it appeared that our com-mitment to the group was waning. Each of us convinced ourselves that our own girlfriend was the one who had broken the mold, and embraced the fantasy that our friends liked these girls in a way they had never liked any of the others. The girls were props in a weird teenage psychodrama. Now, when I see a big group of young guys out with one girl, often bored, often texting, often seated outside the circle of boys (the boyfriend occasionally, sheepishly, making token efforts to include her), I feel sad for her, whose expectations are being lowered every minute she spends being told this is normal.

I came to these understandings slowly and stupidly. When I made new friends in college and grad school and ranted to them about the obnoxious personalities of these other girlfriends, they looked at me like I was unhinged. When they met the girlfriends, after months of stories about their awfulness, they always said, "She seems fine." And I would insist: "No, you have to get to know her. You'll see."

But these people were fine. We were the problem, obviously.

My first relationship was built on a foundation of Instant Message conversations on AOL, where I could be funnier and smarter and sharper than in person. I had a computer in my room, so I could wait online all night (updating my profile relentlessly to include just the right Kurt Vonnegut quote; analyzing the profiles of girls I knew; skimming football discussion forums; lurking in adult chat rooms, too afraid to say anything, but eager to see people talking about sex, sharing their *a/s/l*). When my girlfriend signed on, I waited for her to initiate the conversation because I needed to feel like she *wanted* to talk to me, and more than a few times she took too long to send me a message and I signed off out of spite and laid in my bed for an hour rehearsing awful fights with her. Most nights, I dragged her into endless conversations about my anger and depression. I thought being sad meant being deep, and I thought being deep meant being smart. We often communicated through song lyrics. In person, I was too afraid to try to kiss her or hold her hand or show any specific vulnerability. I was generally nice to her, and I made her laugh, but in no way was I a good boyfriend. A year later, she broke up with me the morning after my junior prom, and I spent the next six months simmering in a rage toward her and anyone who dared to be in a relationship. I wrote a packet of awful poems that I showed to Kevin, even though he has no interest in reading or writing poetry. I wanted him, I guess, to tell me I'd done something beautiful with my pain. Instead he asked, "Are you going to kill yourself?" My ex-girlfriend changed her AOL name to avoid me. I never threatened her, but I also never left her alone. Too often the project of remembering is realizing you were the bad guy when you thought you were the hero.

It is easy for me to picture myself, had I been born 10 years later, sitting in a toxic Reddit forum, or even on 4chan, commiserating with fellow sad teens over how monstrous women are, and how unfair it is to be cursed to live alone. I could have slipped into a place like 8chan, which is a breeding ground for extremism among angry middle-class boys, a fever swamp of misogyny, racism, and irony so thick nobody knows who is really serious until somebody ends up dead. In 2014, a so-called incel named Elliot Rodger went on a killing spree near the campus of UC Santa Barbara because he wanted to get revenge on girls, in general, for his virginity. In his video manifesto, he says, "I don't know why you girls aren't attracted to me, but I will punish you all for it. It's an injustice, a crime... I'm the perfect guy and yet you throw yourselves at these obnoxious men instead of me, the supreme gentleman." Incel forums had started as well-intentioned support groups but mutated into places for young men to stew over being deprived of the sex they were entitled to, to fantasize about violence against Chads and Stacies (essentially the cool kids, their mortal enemies), to talk about being redpilled (having their eyes opened to the true reality, as in *The Matrix*). They are obsessed with testosterone levels and think nothing is more emasculating than having consumed soy or seed oils. Recently, they invented the term "dogpilled," to refer to their belief that beautiful women are having sex with their dogs instead of eligible young men, due to their depravity and shallowness. I don't think we've fully grappled with the extent to which being online has destroyed the minds of so many young people like Rodger. Probably we'll never be able to measure it, because it's not only the extreme cases, but tens of thousands of young men just like him who wanted help and found it in the worst possible places. By the time he was recording his manifesto, nobody in the world could have pulled him out.

Rodger shot 20 people, and now he is a martyr for even more deranged young men who have no idea how to relate to women and sit inside their homes watching countless hours of porn and letting the resentment fester inside them. They post video tributes to him and flood forums with Elliot Rodger memes. Since then, dozens have killed in his name, talking about trying to beat his "high score."

I know all this because I'm online all the time. Some people are more aware of it all because of the gradual mainstreaming of QAnon, the mass murder in Christchurch, the fact that the man who reshaped the entire Republican party in his grotesque image is terminally online, and Facebook having evolved into a wasteland full of fake news stories designed exclusively to wreck people's brains. But it's still largely impenetrable. When I try to explain incels, let alone redpilling or—Christ—dogpilling, normal people look at me like I've lost my mind.

I'm not saying I would have become Elliot Rodger. I'm saying I'm glad I never had the chance to find out. I don't mean to say that the internet was so innocent back then (in AOL chat rooms, there was a thriving child pornography trade, for example). But it felt less decided. The online world still hadn't taken on its true form, and so the possibilities for destruction seemed so remote. Back then, I dealt with my lovesick misery the way most boys did: by listening to Metallica and building elaborate fantasies in which I became rich and famous and those girls all ended up regretting that they'd missed out on me. There was no twisted support group waiting to convince me to commit violence. There was just me and my feelings and a need to find a way out. I'm not nostalgic for any of it. I wish young people now had an alternative.

2000

There is no reason to trust any adult who longs wistfully for high school. That time is bad for everyone, even when it's good. A month after graduation, I would work as an intern for ABC at the Republican National Convention in Philly, where I operated the teleprompter on a live show for Arianna Huffington, because a British freelancer had gone on a cocaine binge and never returned. I didn't know anything about Republicans or Democrats then. I didn't care. I had gotten very good grades throughout school, but I was too wrapped up in myself for it to mean anything.

After kids in Philly graduate, they go down the shore for senior week. They get drunk and get in fights and doggedly pursue sex like the kids in a straight-to-video *American Pie* sequel. So much of our energy at that time was focused on acquiring alcohol and then consuming it without getting in trouble. I always thought that when I got older the novelty of acquiring new beers would wear off and I'd lose interest, but over time it takes on new permutations. You stop sneaking it into the house, but you find new excuses to stock the fridge: a nice summer day, an overpriced limited release, a holiday, a minor professional accomplishment, a Thursday.

Here's the most shameful act my friends and I committed on senior week: on the first day, we found a driver's license that belonged to a 37-year-old Black man named Gary. We joked about using the ID to buy more beer, and over the course of the afternoon, as we downed a case of Corona, it evolved into an actual plan. Our designated funny guy, who would later spend a decade trying to break through as a standup comic, painted his face black with a piece of charcoal, and we walked to the liquor store. The clerk could not stop laughing when she saw him, but she refused to serve us. Our friend in blackface shouted, jivingly, "Is this because I'm Black?" An older man named Leo, with a receding ponytail that reached halfway down his back, enjoyed this performance so much he met us outside and offered to buy us booze. When he asked what we wanted, we told him, "Something good," because we didn't know enough then to have regular orders. That night, we drank TGI Friday's mudslide mix and amaretto and retold the story of our afternoon a hundred times.

I have a picture of my friend with his charcoal-covered face; he's smiling broadly and holding a bottle of mudslide mix in one hand. He's wearing a blue t-shirt that says *McAllister's Plants and Shrubs*, a gift from me after my uncle Ed, the gardener, had given me a surplus of his t-shirts. I'm standing to his right side, and two other friends are on his left, all of us in the same t-shirt. I will not show the photo to you. Had we been in high school now, we would have posted this picture on social media, and within a few hours, our lives would have been upended. They would have led *The Today Show* with it; everyone would have staked out exactly the position they'd been paid to take. A lot of people would have gotten mad at us, but we wouldn't have faced any real trouble, because we were young, middle-class, and white. Some of the most disingenuous creeps in the country would take up our cause against the "woke mob" and say the Left just needs to develop a sense of humor. If we wanted, we could be accepted into the cabal of scumbags and freaks who make up the roster of annual CPAC speakers. If we doubled down on it, maybe even started posting more videos in blackface, we could be on stage at the next Republican Convention. It's an easy game to play, if you're okay hating yourself.

One safe way to describe the story of our afternoon in Ocean City is to say, "Oof, that didn't age well." This phrase is meant to give you a pass. You can use it for any kind of media you once enjoyed, no matter how racist, sexist, or homophobic. You say it while shaking your head, but also smirking a little. This shows you're enlightened and you've grown. I could say I didn't know any better then, but that's bullshit. I knew it was bad, but I didn't care about anything other than my entertainment. It was so easy to be casually cruel. We were caught up in performing for one another, and the only thing that mattered was who could get the most laughs in the meanest possible way. Saying something aged poorly is one way to excuse yourself from having to examine your own complicity. If you keep asking questions, eventually you have to dig into what you're doing now that won't have aged well in 20 years, and that's too fraught for many of us to handle. I'm not afraid of "cancel culture" as it's often discussed. I'm afraid of losing the respect of friends and family who matter to me. A lot of my past didn't age well. I hope I am making a better effort of it—all of it—now.

I had been sort of dating a girl at this time, but she didn't come to Ocean City because a few days before we left, her ex-boyfriend had mailed nude photos of her to her parents, along with a several-page letter detailing their sexual history. She was grounded for the summer, and we didn't talk again until 15 years later when she sent me a Facebook message on my birthday. With that quasi-relationship ended, I found myself pinballing between various girls throughout the week because everyone was drunk and determined to have an experience that felt meaningful. I found that when I was a little bit drunk, people thought I was funny, especially if everyone else was also drunk. I slept in the same bed with one girl, both of us lying rigidly at a distance like kids at an eighth-grade dance. This was my first time ever sleeping in bed with a person not in my family. In the morning, I tried to kiss her and she turned away. We went on a handful of dates over the summer, then spent most of the first semester of college flirting with each other over Instant Messages. I drove to Loyola once to visit her but I found we had forgotten how to speak to each other in person. I left her dorm after a few hours, drove back home, and that night she got drunk and sent me a series of angry messages. "Being rude to people doesn't make you more interesting," she said.

Suppose I had made a different series of choices in my pursuit of her—maybe being more honest and more emotionally available, two moves that were not in my repertoire then—leading to our ending up in a serious relationship. Who knows for how long, if it falls apart due to the distance or if we stay together through college and then try living together in an apartment in Iowa City. It's hard for me to imagine us ever getting beyond a year, even in the best-case scenarios. I have tried to trace the butterfly effect of that alternate path, though. Say we're together for the remainder of freshman year, then break up over the summer. Maybe I still meet LauraBeth and we start dating and eventually get married and everything else remains basically the same. But maybe somewhere in there LauraBeth starts dating someone else. She continues to view my dorm room as "the scary room," with its non-stop drinking and heavy metal music and the sour odor of spilled bong water. We either never meet or never give each other a chance. From there, it's all a mystery. There are too many variables.

Sleeping on the floor of a dingy Ocean City condo, beer bottles scattered everywhere, the sound of an endless game of beer pong clattering in the background, I was seven months from meeting the woman I would eventually marry. We've been together for 23 years; back then, even living another 23 years would have seemed impossible to me.

2001

Sophomore year, I moved with three friends to an off-campus apartment because we were tired of sneaking beer into La Salle's dorms and getting into trouble with the RA (we had already been written up twice and forced to go to alcohol counseling for a semester). We filled a sock drawer with bottles of whiskey and rum, and one roommate brought two pounds of pot, which lasted a couple weeks. Like the college boy stereotypes we were, we maintained a collection of empty bottles on our windowsill, which I periodically rotated and dusted to keep them looking fresh (the whole year, I never cleaned the kitchen or bathroom). I stood sometimes in the courtyard and admired our bottles from the outside, wondering if passersby ever envied us. My world was so small then. All day we told stories about how drunk we had been on previous nights, including meticulous counts of which beers we'd had, and how long it had taken us to drink them. Half of these stories were true and half of those we forgot before we finished telling them.

I had begun dating LauraBeth in February, and I still didn't know how to navigate our relationship. Over the summer, I often borrowed my dad's minivan to drive to her house in Jersey, and though I'd promised to be home by midnight, I would leave after 1 AM, driving home fast enough that I hoped to somehow make time go in reverse (I also got three speeding tickets in two weeks). She had met my parents and I'd met hers, and we were in all ways an official couple. Still, I was afraid my friends would judge me as a sellout if I was with her too much on campus. The last thing I wanted was to be one of those nauseating college couples that spends every moment together, so that they meld into one unwieldy and insecure non-person. I wouldn't commit to specific plans with her, and if we ran into each other at the dining hall, I sat at a table far away. I thought about her constantly, but never said so out loud. The last thing I wanted was for people to think I was in love. She was already the most important person in my life, and she is the most important person in this book. I have now known her longer than I knew my own dad.

I worked Friday nights, taking two buses back home after class for a 5 PM to 1 AM shift at a famous cheesesteak shop, followed by a 10 AM to 5 PM shift on Saturday morning. I got paid $10 per hour under the table, so every Saturday I returned to campus with $170 in my pocket, making me much richer than my friends with work-study jobs. One Friday after classes, LauraBeth invited me back to her dorm, but I told her I wanted to stop by my apartment instead. We got into what I thought was a lighthearted argument about how I was neglecting her, and she started crying for reasons I was too self-absorbed to understand; I took her tears as a personal affront and I wanted to do something to reassert my independence. My roommates were standing across the street waiting for me, so I sprinted toward them, planning on tackling one of them, the most masculine behavior I could think of. Before I reached them, I slipped in a puddle of oil and sprained my ankle badly enough that I could barely stand. I had sprained my ankle many times playing soccer, and I would do so several more times over the ensuing years, but this one was the worst of them all. After sitting with ice on my ankle for a half hour, I was still in enough pain that I had to call out of work. I should have gone to the hospital, and if I had, maybe I wouldn't have spent the next 15 years limping around my house, sometimes afraid to go up the stairs because the pain might be so great that I wouldn't be able to make it.

Throughout my twenties, I assumed I would have to live with this pain—inconsistent, but intense enough that it could drop me to my knees. On vacations, we wandered through strange cities on foot, knowing it was possible I would suddenly be rendered immobile. In 2017, a new pain emerged, a steady burning just above the medial bone. Finally, I saw a doctor, assuming I would need surgery and months of painful rehab and then follow-up surgeries. The doctor said my right deltoid ligament was gone completely, replaced by scar tissue. "No wonder it hurts," he said, pressing on it, making it hurt. But there was no surgery required. After one steroid injection and five weeks of physical therapy, I was pain-free for the first time since college. It was so easy I couldn't believe it.

After I called out of work the day of the sprain, we decided to throw a party to celebrate my first Friday night ever on campus. We got our beer from a corner store in the neighborhood where nobody checked ID and we had to slide a pile of bills through a slot in bulletproof glass six inches thick. You could get 40-ounce bottles of Olde English for $3.50 each if you were feeling fancy, but you could get Private Stock for $2.50 and Country Club for $2. The cops didn't care about underage kids buying beer because they had bigger problems to worry about in North Philly. The guys playing basketball across the street didn't care about us either; we were just tourists in their world, and next year we would be replaced by some new kids trying to recreate a Dr. Dre video in their dorms.

I was drunk by five, when my shift would have started. Laura-Beth came over before most of the other guests, still upset with me but also concerned about my ankle. I have a picture of her from that night holding a bottle of Olde E, and she's smiling more comfortably than she does in most pictures from that time. She looks relaxed and happy. Probably she was very worried, about my pain, about the noise we were making, about my self-destructiveness, but she'd gotten very good at hiding it already. If you look long enough at a picture, you can see whatever you want.

What happened at the party doesn't matter. What matters is the ankle, and the damage we do to ourselves because we think it's funny and we're too young to care what happens next. You do stupid things and 20 years later your body lives with the consequences, the aching knees and the creaky neck and the damaged heart. Your funny stories become throbbing reminders of your mortality. The ghosts live inside your bad bones.

At one of my final physical therapy appointments, I was rocking on a balance board, training my body to stand correctly, and listening to two elderly women discuss their ailments. The conversation had begun with one woman saying, "You look good," and the other responding: "I look like yesterday's meatloaf." She talked about her physical breakdown, how hard it was to build enough strength to lift her feet over minor obstacles, how she could feel her vertebrae grinding together. "Sometimes I try to explain it and all my words leave me," she said.

The first woman changed the subject to men, their unreliability and general badness. Her husband had died years ago and she was glad he was dead. Another man at her senior living complex had been rude to her that morning. "So you know me: I gave him two fuck yous. That's the only way to handle it." She looked at one of the young female trainers. "If some man gives you trouble, you give him two fuck yous. One is not enough."

The second woman followed with a story about being young and stuck in traffic with a man she didn't love. "I was so mad at everyone, and I didn't know what to do. So I got right up out of that car. I told him fuck you and then I walked up to the intersection. There was a cop on one of those police horses, and I started cursing that horse out on the spot." She wrapped a resistance band around the arch of her foot and pulled. "That was the last time I ever let a man treat me like that. And I never liked horses anyway."

What I'm saying is: if I hadn't slipped in oil back then, maybe I never would have heard this conversation, and what would have been the point of a life without it?

2002

In summer, we played Wiffle Ball. A few nights a week, we met at Shawmont, a public school that had a big playground with a map of the U.S. painted onto the concrete. It was far enough away from any houses that nobody complained about the noise we made, and the fence was a perfect distance for measuring home runs. We walked to 7-11 and loaded up on Combos and Snapple. Between games we argued about sports, especially fantasy sports. Now and then, a cop rolled by, saw a bunch of kids with bats, and gave us a warning not to cause any trouble, but you could tell his heart wasn't in it.

My friends had dispersed across eight colleges, and these were the last years when you could live in a different place from someone and not know anything about their life. There were IM conversations and away messages, but it wasn't the same. Only some of us had cell phones, and text messages were expensive. Email still felt weird. In May, we reconvened and tried to fit in as much time together as we could. I wouldn't appreciate until later that these were the last gasps of our collective friendship. Though everyone in the group still lives in the area, I only see one of the other guys occasionally. I'm friends with a few on Facebook, but I only go on there when I have something to promote.

One night, someone brought two bottles of Jack Daniel's, and after a couple hours, we got loud and sloppy, and the cops chased us off. After I got caught in a sudden downpour, I ended up hitching a ride home with a woman who had just left her shift as a stripper in Kensington, a Philly neighborhood infamous for its crime and drugs. I was reckless enough then to get into anyone's car. Six months later, when I didn't want to walk to work in the snow, I hopped in a van driven by two middle-aged people who were drinking Schnapps from the bottle and having what they called a "snow party." They crashed into a snowbank a half-mile from my work and I got out while they tried to get the van back on the road. The stripper who picked me up wanted to know where to buy crack, but I did not know where to buy crack, an answer she did not believe or accept.

There's a lot more to this story, but the ending is unsatisfying. It's all details without a purpose. Three years later, in grad school, I would write a 10,000-word short story about this incident. I was so proud of it that I used it as my submission for a prestigious fellowship, and I spent 50 dollars mailing it to top-tier literary journals. A few minutes ago, I reread the first page and it was so bad I stopped breathing. I can't imagine how I spent months (*months!*) crafting this story, certain that strangers would care. That they would *pay* to print it. I feel a great retroactive shame at having forced my peers to read it, at having made a postal worker carry it on their back. A more optimistic person would see this shame as a sign of the progress I've made as a writer. A more optimistic person would make all kinds of healthy choices I don't make.

My closest friend from first grade until the end of college was a guy I'll call James. I slept at his house most Fridays, had Roy Rogers for dinner with his family. We shared every inside joke and every first experience. We listened to the same music and ate the same foods and got in fights with the same guys. When I moved to Iowa City for grad school, he and another friend named Ian drove in the U-Haul with me, and that evening, while Ian slept, James drank most of a bottle of vodka and hugged me and asked me why I wasn't sad. "It's all over," he said, and I laughed at him for being too drunk and dramatic.

By the end of college, when we all drank together—besides watching football, this was the only reason we saw each other— all we talked about were stories that had happened long before.

We didn't create new memories; we tried to enshrine the old ones by repeating the old stories until we had them memorized. We'd talked about my hitchhiking with the stripper a thousand times. There was nothing left but the past.

After grad school, LauraBeth and I got engaged and then bought a house in New Jersey. James came to visit; we sat in fold-out stadium chairs and watched a Flyers game and ate pizza and talked about almost nothing. A year later, we met for cheesesteaks at my old workplace, barely speaking. I would be the best man at his wedding a year later and have seen him only one time since. The wedding is the line of demarcation, the last time you really see most of your old friends. They're partying on your dime because they know this is the end.

LauraBeth—who has had the same best friend since first grade and has marked the birthdays of seemingly every person she has ever known on our calendar—sometimes encourages me to email him (I can't do that; he never told me his email address). To at least send a text (he hasn't responded to a text in five years). She says I should ask if we can grab lunch again. I should tell him I'd like to meet his son. Is it bad if I say I don't see the point? Whoever James is today, there's a good chance we would not get along at all, except by riding on the wave of nostalgia and sports talk. He's a cop and the son of a veteran and has always held militaristic and authoritarian views. It's not a stretch for me to imagine him looking, say, at a video of South American children cruelly locked in cages along the U.S. border and saying something like, "If they didn't want to get arrested they shouldn't have broken the law." Or maybe a pleasant conversation gets derailed when he says opioid addicts deserve to die because they're stupid enough to get addicted in the first place. I suspect even in 2002 if we'd been paying any attention, we would have fought bitterly about the Bush administration and the torture memos and Abu Ghraib. Now, the divide feels insurmountable. I worry that if we met each other for the first time today, we could end up in an actual fistfight. It wouldn't be the first time we'd fought, but fists are heavier when you're older. Punches land harder, and they're not so easy to forget.

I've slipped into writing fiction (this happens every time, I can never stay on track), because I don't know who he is now, and we're never going to talk about it. I have wondered sometimes if he would come to my funeral. Or if I would go to his. I admit it makes me sad to type these sentences. When I was young, I thought the only way to validate a friendship was for it to last forever. On campus, I see the undergrads sometimes taking 10 minutes to say goodbye to one another; they are savoring the moment and ensuring that everyone knows, no matter what, they will be back. It used to take me an hour to leave a party because I needed to individually say goodbye to every friend, even though I would see them the next day. Now I walk away and trust everyone will eventually figure out I'm gone.

With each year that passes, each friendship that fades, each new connection that flares up briefly, it has become so much easier to not say goodbye, to just leave. You can't survive in this world alone but you can't hold on to the same people forever. It's not fair to them. Every draft you write is progress toward some other better version of the project you're working on. Nobody writes a new book; they write the same book over and over until they feel a little better about it.

2003

I sit with two of my roommates, watching the news coverage of the invasion of Iraq, aired uncritically and stupidly, the same way they would broadcast the Rose Parade, all of the commentary indistinguishable from ad copy about the immense might of the American military and the necessity of an invasion, all of it scripted by ghouls who will prove to be grifters and criminals but will nonetheless 10 years later be treated as honorable statesmen despite no particular effort on their part to rehabilitate their image, having simply been redeemed by the passage of time and the more overt awfulness of their political descendants; there are people dying on the screen but we're told to focus on the spectacular explosions, which, if I'm being honest, a bad part of me does find enthralling, and it becomes too easy to detach myself from the reality that an illegal and ill-conceived war—these are not observations made in hindsight, both of these problems were obvious then to anyone who was being honest—has begun for no specific reason beyond a general desire for vengeance, which means thousands will be slaughtered in the short term, and none of us realizes this war will continue forever, that it will lurch forward year after year justifying its own existence because once war has started it's really easy to explain why you need to keep warring, especially when there is no specific end goal that would generally be accepted as winning, and the ripple effects of wanton bombing lead to economic and cultural devastation, to regional destabilization, and therefore more terror, and after a while most people will be able to go weeks at a time without ever considering the lives of the soldiers abroad or the citizens of the occupied lands, war is an abstraction, a concept we salute before football games right after we express our awareness of breast cancer, and when the soldiers come back from the war we say thank you for your service and maybe they go viral by surprising their kid by showing up at their graduation or something, and we all feel great about it. Our hearts are warmed.

Prior to this year, I had not earned my cynicism. A variety of systemic biases and supports had allowed me to live 21 years without really having to understand anything. None of my friends cared about politics or social justice because caring about other people was extremely uncool (this attitude is markedly different from the students I teach now, who aren't all thoughtful and well-read, but are dramatically more aware of the world around them than we were). Even though La Salle was run by Christian Brothers and ostensibly pursued a mission of public service, this commitment rarely trickled down to the students. What I wanted to do then was play *Madden* on PlayStation 2. My roommates and I stayed up until 3 AM playing game after game, hurling controllers across the room and screaming at the TV and punching holes in the wall when we lost. There wasn't time for anything else.

That semester I took a course on Dietrich Bonhoeffer and the Nazi resistance, in addition to an independent study on the literature of the Holocaust. A semester later, I took a course on the 1960s with a man named John Raines, who was a genuine Civil Rights hero—Freedom Rider, organizer of numerous marches and prayer vigils, and one of the co-conspirators who robbed the FBI field offices and exposed COINTELPRO. For the first time in my life, I was asked to engage critically with systemic injustice. Like many college students, I became unbearably smug about my political awakening, but that doesn't mean I was wrong. A year later, when La Salle closed a major thoroughfare in our North Philly community because they said it was too dangerous for the students to walk across, I wrote an op-ed for the school paper accusing the university and its students of abandoning their high-minded mission in favor of classism and racism. The University President invited me to his office to discuss my article, but when I heard how angry he was, I no-showed, and spent the rest of my time at the school avoiding him. I never wrote for the paper again.

My dad died a couple months after the shock and awe attacks. While he was dying, I struggled with my independent study more severely than any other school project I had undertaken; my professor expected more of me than I was able to deliver. I quit my job just to feel agency over something, and three months later, my rent check bounced. At my friend James' 21st birthday party, I got beaten up in a bar fight, thrown through a table and kicked in the chest hard enough that I had boot prints in my skin the next day. I don't even know why we'd been fighting; I saw my friends getting punched and decided to make myself punchable too. I started applying to grad schools even though I had no interest in going. The war continued, possibly through the rest of my life. It was a time of extraordinary, ceaseless shame. I spent so much of it feeling like I should be doing something besides whatever I was doing.

There's this writing move I feel like I'm expected to do here, at the end of an essay, where I add some flourishes and assign meaning or reveal hidden beauty in the events I'm describing, but sometimes there is no meaning, and the only beauty or ugliness is what's on the surface. What am I supposed to tell you? That everything got better? Come on.

2004

My first niece was born shortly before I flew home from Iowa City for winter break from grad school. We did what families do after a child is born: everyone sat in a circle and stared at her, waiting for any movement to overanalyze. People cooed her name, over and over. People said she looks like her father or her mother or her grandmother or whoever they wanted her to look like. Her skull wasn't even fully formed; she was a wrinkly, screaming mass, and she terrified me. My mom wanted to take a picture of me holding her, but I refused, so instead Kevin held her and sat next to me. I worried I would have dropped her, sure, but I also worried that once she was in my arms I would suddenly find myself wanting a child of my own, the kind of stupid epiphany movie characters have all the time.

I had stressed to LauraBeth early in our relationship that I did not want children. She didn't either, but people change their minds. Biology takes over. I had convinced myself that despite what she'd told me, she would wake up one morning and give me an ultimatum: I could have her with children, or I could have nobody. I don't know what choice I would have made. Either one would have felt unfair, to everyone.

Kevin and his wife had another daughter two years later, and LauraBeth's brothers now have two young children each. Our house is about 60 percent baby-proofed because we want friends to trust that they can bring their kids over without risking their lives. Every October, as long as we have lived together, we have hosted a big pumpkin carving party, with up to 60 guests, and over the past five years, it has evolved into an event at which half the attendees are under 10 years old and most people are gone by 8 PM. Near the end of one recent party, I was helping a group of kids get settled on the couch with Cheerios and juice and blankets so they could watch *Monsters, Inc.* and when they were all settled, a friend said, "I can't believe I am watching Tom talk to kids." Because I was more callous when I was younger, I gave people the impression that I am one of those lunatics who harbor animosity toward parents in general, those people you can find online who use terms like "crotch goblins" to describe children, and I have exerted a great deal of energy reassuring friends that their kids are welcome in my house. LauraBeth has worked at a children's hospital for 20 years, and anyway she has a more intuitive sense of how to deal with children, but I can affirm that I am now someone you can leave alone with your kid(s) and trust that they will be returned safely and perhaps even having had fun.

Though our families celebrate holidays together, and in 2022 we all traveled together with my mom to Ireland, I still have a distant relationship with my nieces. As far as I know, they don't dislike me but we do not really know each other. I was living in the Midwest when they were babies and we never formed any specific bond. To blame it on geography is dishonest, though. The reason I don't have a meaningful relationship with Kevin's kids is because I never tried to have one, and now that they're both in their late teens, it all seems calcified.

LauraBeth's brother's children love her, and they like me, which is not bad, considering. They sleep at our house sometimes, and they play games with me, and they greet me at the door when I visit their house. I'm sure Kevin wonders where this relatively fun uncle was when his kids were young. I was more wrapped up in my own life then. I didn't know how to talk to kids and I didn't bother to learn.

My oldest niece has started college and is moving into adulthood, and I think she looks increasingly like I did at that age. She's a gifted and driven artist, and I hope for her sake that that's where the similarities between us end. I hope she has the confidence I never had, and that she loves herself in a way I never really learned to do. Her younger sister recently surprised everyone by announcing she wants to go to college to become a writer, and, after some prodding by her parents, she asked me to give her feedback on a packet of stories. Lately, both nieces have been more eager to join the adult conversations instead of withdrawing with a phone or a sketchpad, and I think they are learning that I can be sometimes funny. As I get older, I feel the distance between myself and the rest of my family more acutely. I try writing about it because if I arrange the words in the right order, maybe I can summon into existence the world I prefer.

Six years ago, I was flying home from a writing conference in Green Bay. Despite my best efforts to look unapproachable, the man next to me asked what book I was reading. It was Erica Jong's novel *Fear of Flying*, which I assured him was just a coincidence and not a comedy bit, which assurance only confused him more than if I'd said nothing at all. I didn't want to talk about books. I had been in town promoting my novel; I didn't want him to know I was an author, and I especially didn't want him to know my book was about gun violence and misogyny. Two hours is a long time to talk about such topics. I could tell by his relief pitcher goatee and the Ray-Bans tucked into his shirt pocket and the over earnest way he maintained eye contact for just a second too long that he was a specific type of conservative man who would not share my values, and would in fact have no respect for my work (later, he would complain, unprompted and at great length, about how the liberal media is "out to get" nuclear power plants).

Because he would not accept silence as an option, eventually I explained why I was traveling. He politely skimmed the jacket copy on my novel. "How about that?" he said to his teenage daughter. "A real living writer!" People are usually impressed to meet writers even if they don't read books or care about writing. They are impressed by the act of someone having written. In a different situation, I would have tried to make a sale, but there was no way.

Mid-flight, he asked if I had children. He asked why not, then he asked again. "I don't want children," is a valid answer. It's the end of a conversation. If you push me, I'll tell you I feel an existential despair about the future of the planet, of humans in general. I am intensely protective of my time and my space. Children are expensive. And also: my dad was 54 when he died and LauraBeth's mother was 49. We have spent our entire adult lives certain we will die young. I could have told this man that LauraBeth had recently had her fallopian tubes removed to reduce her risk of ovarian cancer, but instead I said something about how it's a big decision and it's just not the right time. I asked him about his own kids to distract him, and I learned the daughter was one of his 13 children. "We are proud Roman Catholics," he said. He grabbed my arm. "Tom, I can tell you're a good Roman Catholic, too. Listen: every man has one opportunity in this world to become a great man. I know it's scary. But when you get home, you tell your wife it's time for you to start making babies." What I didn't say: pursuing greatness is what ruins people. I'm trying to be adequate and relatively safe and go to bed without feeling too guilty.

Another thing I didn't say: what kind of fucking speech is that? Who told you this is how to act in public?

To his daughter he said, "You never know. We might be angels sent to save him from this path." I'd like to think that if I meet an angel, it won't be while I'm flying coach from Green Bay to Philly. I'd like to think an angel would know enough to let me read my book, but I guess angels are pushy like that. They have a job to do too. Until you earn your wings, they start you off with low-priority tasks like pestering some guy on a plane about his kids. Later, they give you a sword and let you fight the demons.

2005

In February, LauraBeth flew to Iowa City to visit me for my birth-day. It was colder there than I had ever thought possible—neg-ative 30 degrees, factoring in wind chill. The kind of cold that would kill a Martian. The college students still went out at night in short skirts and t-shirts, because they didn't want their jackets to smell like smoke. These two years in Iowa City were the last time in my life when I would know what it felt like to sit in a bar with dozens of smokers, lit cigarettes glowing like alligators' eyes in the dark, smoke snaking its way into my lungs and my hair and my clothing forever.

I didn't have to pay for utilities in my apartment, so I set the thermostat to 80 and we quarantined ourselves in the greenhouse heat. My mom had mailed me a care package that included authen-tic cheesesteaks, Tastykakes, and a birthday banner, which we hung above the couch. We ate chicken parm and an ice cream cake, and we watched the NBA All-Star skills competition on the new TV she had bought me that morning. We'd driven together to Best Buy to pick up a 27-inch flat screen, replacing the one I'd owned since I was 15. This was now the fanciest TV I had ever owned, though it was still a monstrous tube model so big it didn't fit in my hatch-back. We removed it from the box at the store, crammed into the trunk, and drove home with hazard lights flashing and the rear windshield flapping in the wind like a ridiculous mouth laughing at us the whole way. I lived on the second floor, and carrying that TV up a narrow, winding flight of stairs was my greatest physical achievement of 2005. I preferred watching sports to engaging in them. I was gaining weight again rapidly, and people kept saying things like, "You've really filled out," which is only meant as a compliment when you say it to toddlers or rescue dogs.

Sports have always been a central fact of my life, but never more so than my two years in Iowa City—they were the one interest that helped me still feel connected to home when I was alone in my apartment and feeling like a failure as a writer and a teacher— and so I was as invested in the dunk contest as anyone in the country that night. This is the point where, if I've had a few drinks and a somewhat willing audience, I would spend the next hour demanding justice for Andre Iguodala, who was robbed of the dunk contest title that year. This is also where I would complain about Nate Robinson getting unlimited attempts to hit his final dunk. But I'm trying to get better about that kind of thing. I realize nobody cares.

LauraBeth grew up with two athletic and ultra-competitive brothers, and through a combination of genetics, conditioning, and sheer force of will, she now harbors an antipathy to competition that is healthier than my worldview but is, frankly, a little unnerving. She played field hockey in high school, but never felt any particular drive to win. She will not play board games or engage in other competitions with the rest of the family because of how much she hated all of it when she was young. She watches sports with me but can't help feeling badly for the losing team after the final whistle (even if it's a team we all justifiably hate, like the Dallas Cowboys). She asks me to change the channel so we can look away from their sagging shoulders and heartbroken faces; she sees them not as enemies, but as young men, some young enough they can't even legally drink, enduring one of the worst moments of their lives. Though this is not remotely how I live or think, I understand it to be an admirable trait. All of which is to say, exhibition sports are the ideal environment for her. The guys in the dunk contest, like every pro athlete, are pathologically competitive, but they are having fun and there are no real consequences for losing.

I want to clarify something: dunks matter more than you think they do. You may want to tell me it's all a big dumb spectacle and the scoring doesn't make sense, and it's just a show to sell Sprite and sneakers, and yes, sure, that's what it is. But strip all the nonsense away and you see an aesthetic achievement that can only be performed by a tiny percentage of humans in world history. Each dunk is one of the most perfect sporting feats on the planet, a beautiful expression of athletic perfection, of power, speed, and creativity. These players—their bodies built specifically for this task, spinning in the goddamn air, not just floating because there's violence propelling it, and throwing it down behind their heads with more grace and fluidity in the coordination than many dancers—are the culmination of a century worth of training, learning, and evolutionary adaptations. Major sports leagues should take themselves less seriously anyway. What's more ridiculous than watching a group of NFL men in a TV studio, wearing suits and standing on a fake field while they shout about honor and duty? It's one of the worst aspects of our culture. Events like the dunk contest puncture the veneer of self-importance that covers every major league. They remind people that this is dumb and the dumbness is what makes it fun.

A couple years after I moved back to the East Coast and we bought a house and got married, we finally bought another new TV, upgrading to HD, which helped us more clearly see the anguish on the faces of the losing teams. The TV from my 23rd birthday was transferred to the attic, and then when we moved again it went to the basement of the new house, and, finally, we hauled it out to the curb, where it sat for a week before I learned that this is not how you dispose of a TV anymore (on any given day in the suburbs, sidewalks are dotted with hulking tube TVs like meteors crashed to earth). I could have left it on the curb for years. Eventually I would drag some old furniture out there and that would stay too and soon our whole living room could be on the sidewalk, a mirror of the lives we tried to hide inside.

Because our house is full of toxic materials the township won't collect, we drove one afternoon with a trunk full of paint cans, dangerous solvents, batteries, and the TV to the landfill in Pennsauken, New Jersey. I wrote a research paper on landfills in high school biology, but I don't get the science behind them, whether there is anything more to it than digging a giant hole and filling it with garbage until the earth is too full and then you move down the road to a new hole. Once it's out of my sight, I trust that it is someone else's problem. All this stuff was alive once and you expect it to smell like death, but it smells like nothing (the landfill itself has a 5-star rating on Google, with the top review stating, "It don't even smell"). We dropped our trash in the appropriate areas, ending at a walk-in dumpster, a container for obsolete electronics. Inside, piled floor to ceiling, were TVs and computer monitors. The foundation of these stacks was several vintage console TVs, each of which I imagined having been passed down through their families when they became too unwieldy to move anymore. Maybe they trundled through thrift stores and flea markets, through the homes of various well-meaning people planning to fix them up and turn them into a cool showpiece in their art school loft, but eventually they were hauled to this spot.

Being in the center of a county dump is humbling and a little upsetting. It is a reminder that even if, like me, you think of yourself as being a minimalist, most people are surrounded by garbage. It's all disposable and you're disposable too. It's all replaceable and you're replaceable too. In 2005, this TV was the center of my world, and now it would be piled, for the rest of the life of the planet, in this dumpster in Pennsauken. It would outlive me by a million years, and that whole time it would be utterly useless, just plastic and wires, there forever.

2006

The tornado siren stood a 10th of a mile from my apartment, so I always knew when we were in danger. For most of my two years in Iowa City, my friends laughed at my fear, but that didn't stop me from googling tornado survival tips at night. Back home, I'd experienced a couple of earthquakes so minor that some people never noticed them, some heavy rains from dying hurricanes, and a number of blizzards and ice storms. These events could be inconvenient, but they never threatened to kill me like a tornado would. Everyone in my MFA program repeated the conventional wisdom that the Iowa River was a natural protection against tornadoes, which allegedly couldn't jump over water. They said it often enough that I think they believed it, though it was obviously wrong. Feeling safe sometimes means forgetting the facts and embracing the right set of comfortable delusions.

One night the sirens wailed and kept wailing, and on TV they showed a map of Iowa's counties with every block in the southeast corner colored a deep red. The meteorologist said people in Johnson County should seek shelter immediately. I texted Laura-Beth, a thousand miles away, to tell her I was afraid—she'd stayed in New Jersey when I moved to grad school, and we were now both counting the days till I could come home—and then I sought shelter. I'd read that one option for sheltering during a tornado was to lie down in the bathtub with a mattress over top like a lid on a stock pot. I put some snacks, a can of beer, and a battery-powered radio that my mom had mailed specifically for this situation into the tub and then dragged my mattress from the bedroom. The bathroom was so small my mattress didn't fit through the door. I left the snacks, beer, and mattress and decided to go to the building's basement with my radio instead. My neighbor across the hall opened his door at the exact time I opened mine. He was about my age and we had never spoken to one another, but we agreed to go downstairs together.

Two weeks later, I heard a woman's screams from his apartment. More than an argument; actual terror like I'd never heard in real life before. Monitoring the hall through my peephole, I saw his door swing open and a naked woman charge out, clutching a t-shirt against her chest. From my window overlooking the parking lot, I saw a van pull in as she rushed down the stairs, the back door sliding open, and the naked woman jumping in. They were back on Route 1 before the door closed. Through the peephole I watched my neighbor step into the hallway, look around stunned for a minute, and then return to his apartment. I never saw the woman again. Wishing it was something besides what it obviously was, I did not call the police. I concocted a dozen rationalizations. It's one thing to read about crimes like this, and another to be within a few feet as it unfolded. LauraBeth would ask why I'd never noticed any fighting across the hall before, and why I didn't do anything at all to help, but I had no answers. The day of the tornado, I had no idea my neighbor was the kind of man who would abuse a woman so badly she'd stage a daring breakout in the night, but you never know that, do you? The real problem is any kind of man could be that kind. There's no reconciling the two experiences—the tornado and the woman's escape—but I can't disentangle them in my memory. One night the sirens, and another night the screaming, different kinds of warnings for different kinds of damage. It's easy to become inured to anything if you live close enough to it for long enough. I was 24 and so lost in my own anxieties I rarely took the time to notice anyone else.

The basement doubled as a small laundry room. Four other people were wedged in there by the time we arrived, and I found a seat on top of a dryer. One woman cradled her cat like a baby while her partner played *Sonic the Hedgehog* on his Game Gear with the volume turned all the way up. I set my radio up in the center of the room, and we learned a powerful tornado—later classified as an F2, with winds ranging from 113 to 157 miles per hour—had in fact jumped the river and was rampaging toward us.

What I remember most is the hail, the machine gun bombardment of ice balls on the roof. One guy ran outside in the hail to check on his car, and I felt like I was living in the scene of a movie just before the most tragic moment, but he came back inside a minute later, unhurt. He announced, "Fucking hail is huge, man," and he shook his head like we should have warned him. On the radio, a reporter said the Walmart had been hit. "There is no looting yet," he added. "I repeat: nobody is looting." Like he was rooting for it to happen.

I texted LauraBeth to tell her I loved her, and then I turned off my phone to preserve the battery. The power in the building flickered off a few times, but when we got the all clear on the radio 30 minutes later, everything was working fine. My car was somehow not damaged by the hail. I hadn't died or even come close to it. The tornado devastated parts of the city, and in the next days, everyone wandered around the city gawking at the damage: dumpsters dropped in the middle of the road, cars bobbing in the river, a sorority building stripped of its façade like a dollhouse. One of the professors in the MFA program scolded us for treating the wreckage as spectacle. But it *was* spectacle. There's nothing more human than emerging from your shelter to look in awe at the damage the planet can do to you.

Did I feel vindicated for having spent two years afraid? I did not. I felt more afraid than before. The fear hadn't done anything to help me. Five days later, I bought an engagement ring at the Coralville Mall. I wasn't planning on it then. The decision had nothing to do with the tornado or facing my mortality. While eating breakfast one morning I realized: Of course I'm going to marry her. Why shouldn't we do it now? There wasn't a moment of doubt. As soon as the thought presented itself to me, I understood what I wanted the rest of my life to be.

In the immediate aftermath of the tornado, I turned my phone back on to let LauraBeth know I was alive, and I saw that I'd received a dozen texts from classmates. Within an hour, I drifted over to a friend's house, where there was no power, but there was a great backyard and a strangely beautiful evening sky. Every few minutes, someone else showed up carrying a random assortment of beer and perishable goods. Because so many people had lost power, they wanted to clear out their fridges, so we were having a feast. Every familiar face was another friend who was safe and another reason to celebrate. Some had sustained real damage to their homes, and at least one guy lost his car—literally, it was on a different block from where he'd parked it. At two in the morning, we were still shoving more and more food inside us, opening one last beer and then one more last beer. We swelled with the urgency of people living their last night on Earth. On one side of the tornado had been grad school and on the other side was the rest of my life, as if it had picked us all up in a single swipe and plopped us all down into some better place. Within a month, I would be gone and I would never speak to most of these people again. For one night, we were all still there. We told the stories of our sheltering experience over and over. I was upstairs and then I was downstairs. It was quiet and then it was so loud. Afterward, I was fine. It all felt impossible.

2007

After two years of teaching as a grad student with no training or oversight, I landed adjunct positions at two colleges in Philly. I was still a mediocre teacher, but I had a degree from a prestigious program and I had experience; colleges are so desperate for cheap labor they will take chances on anyone for a semester. College had been easy for me, so I never paid much attention to what my professors had done. It took me almost a decade to understand the challenges of students who were struggling to stay afloat.

Because I had been a grade-obsessed student, I felt intense guilt about giving any grade worse than a B+ on an assignment. I often inflated grades because I didn't have the courage of my convictions. Part of me knew it was unfair for freshmen to have their GPAs ruined by a class in which they were getting poor leadership and no coherent instruction. Part of me didn't want to deal with the confrontation, to become the bad guy. It was so important to me then that my students liked me (every August, the same nightmare crops up—I'm in front of the classroom and asking questions but no one is listening or even pretending to care, and the more I scream at them to show me respect, the more they laugh at me, and eventually I either storm out of the room or they walk out in protest). When I returned papers, I used to leave them on the desk at the front of the room for the students to pick up on their way out, and while they sorted through the pile, I sneaked away and hustled out of the building. Once, a student who got a B- on an essay melted down in front of the room before I could escape, bawling about how she needed a 3.5 GPA to get into veterinary school, how mean I was to everyone, how stupid the class was in the first place. Confronted with such a raw display of emotion, I said nothing and waited until she collected herself enough to leave the room. She filed a complaint against me, but upon review the department determined that a B- had been an overly generous grade. I hadn't discriminated; I had set her up for failure by teaching nothing specific and grading based on loosely defined criteria.

Before grad school, a former professor had told me that my only job was to write, and never to let any other responsibilities get in the way. I followed his advice halfway, in that I didn't take teaching seriously, but I also did very little writing. Now that I was an adjunct, teaching was no longer something that had happened to me accidentally, but rather a position I'd specifically applied for. I still didn't know what I was doing, but I was *trying*. On the rare occasions when I gave students mediocre grades, I wrote very long notes, encouraging them, explaining how they could improve, justifying myself. One class period, I handed a C+ paper back to a student who was a nice guy but utterly unprepared for college. My note was nearly a page long, and also the most earnest page I've ever written. I had spent the morning dreading giving him this paper.

His eyes widened, then he turned to his friend and punched him in the shoulder. "C+, bitch!" he shouted. They high-fived and left the room.

This memory is lodged so deeply in my mind it will be the last thought I ever process. I will be dying, hooked up to a cluster of tubes and machines, and surrounded by loved ones saying their final goodbyes. I will shout "C+, bitch!" before drawing my final breaths. They will puzzle over my meaning. Later, they'll pretend I'd said something more profound.

I failed enough students that semester (12 out of 36) that I emailed my department chair to ask what a normal number of failures was (His response: "It really depends on the quality of the students"). I felt intense guilt about failing them, especially once I learned about the strong correlation between failing freshman composition and dropping out of college, of student debt and low earnings potential and everything else. Now that I teach full-time at a large state university, most of my students are burdened with complicated backgrounds: low-income families, undocumented parents, disabilities, poor high school preparation. Big schools take in thousands of children every year, brag about their record class sizes, and then toss them into the ocean and see what happens. I am the only authority figure on campus who will know most of my students' names during their first year, which means if they drop out, I am the only one here who will ever remember them. They get placed into one of 150 sections of composition based on the whims of an advisor, and then find out whether they'll have someone like me now—an experienced, invested professor who knows what he's doing—or someone like me from 2007—a frightened, unprepared guy who takes every mistake the students make as a personal attack.

This is what people want to talk to me about when they learn I'm an English professor:

- Books they hated in school
- The one big grammar rule they almost certainly misunderstand but cling to like a lifebuoy for some reason
- The various books they have at one time considered writing, but haven't written
- Everything they think is wrong with lazy and entitled students these days

None of these are good conversations, obviously. People take great pride in being better than the generation after them, especially if they don't know anything about that generation. Acquaintances assume I secretly hate the students, and they keep giving me prompts, inviting me to trash them.

Listen: there are a lot of kids in college who aren't prepared. There are a lot of kids who are irresponsible, who write poorly, who have only the slimmest knowledge of history or literature or religion or civics. There are lots of kids who are getting drunk and high and missing deadlines, maybe not in that order. The number of shameless dead uncle and sick dog emails on deadline nights is consistent and incredible. Almost everyone is on their phones and their computers too much. In 2007, I would never have believed myself saying this, but I genuinely like these students, with their messiness and their drama and their irresponsibility. The whole point is for me to help them navigate a stressful, challenging time in their lives and give them the tools to come out on the other side a little better prepared, a little more open-minded, a little more skilled.

Some of us had the luxury of being annoying within the context of a system that basically made sense. You went to school and got a degree and maybe money was tight through your 20s, but eventually you were doing fine and you could accumulate wealth. My students are acutely aware that college has become a bad financial bet, but it's the only bet they know to make. They trust me to help them improve their odds just a little bit. So I'm going to go to cocktail parties and trash them for reaching out? What kind of person would that make me?

I was exactly that kind of person when I started teaching. Now I'm some other kind of person, and if I'm writing about the most important event of 2007 for me, I have to tell you that's the year I got married. We went to San Francisco on our honeymoon. We went to Napa and drank wine. It was a beautiful time. We were so young we had no idea what we were doing. I look at the pictures and I still recognize both of us. We went up in a hot air balloon and from high above we looked down at a field of sundried tomatoes, and it was the reddest thing I'd ever seen. You've never seen something so red.

2008

It felt for a couple years like we were going to a wedding every week. If not a wedding, then a bachelor(ette) party or a bridal shower, or an engagement party. Once we went to a gender reveal party, which is a party where you find out what gender a cake is, and then people say things like, "I thought it was going to be blue, but it turned out to be pink," or vice versa. Some weekends we went to the ceremony for one wedding and then rushed out to make the reception for another. I ate a lot of platters of above-average chicken with wild rice. It cost the hosts at least $90 to feed us every time. I developed strong feelings regarding wedding favors and seating arrangements. I drank 7 & 7s at the open bars, because they were quick and easy and it felt like the kind of classy drink a guy at a wedding would have ordered two generations ago. We made small talk with the friends of co-workers and the less-beloved aunts and uncles of the bride. I danced with LauraBeth, but not enough; we're both too self-conscious. For years, I harbored this fantasy of secretly taking dance classes for months and then breaking out the killer moves at a wedding, like a sitcom husband from the 1990s, but I never did anything to make this fantasy come to fruition.

We were still young enough to feel obligated to show up any time someone invited us. It would be another 10 years before I finally felt comfortable not going to parties, which has been one of the most liberating feelings of my life. Not going anywhere: the true joy of aging.

Our own wedding was relatively small—75 guests—and about a third of those people are out of our lives now. Kevin was my best

100

man, as I was for him, and my mom spent nearly the entire night on the dance floor (Kevin's wedding was only a couple months after my dad died, and my mom now says she barely remembers it, was trying to get through the day without falling apart).

It's hard to say what the point of the party is. Twenty thousand dollars, for what? I don't know any married couples who wish they'd spent more time or money on their wedding, but everyone keeps doing it.

One of the weddings we attended was for a childhood friend—I'll call him Clark—who I hadn't seen since college. He had dropped out of school and focused exclusively on partying, and by the time most of us graduated, he'd found a new group of friends who had easy access to Xanax and Percocet. Now and then he would borrow money from us, and once he tried to guilt trip me into letting him borrow my credit card so that he could buy a PlayStation. "It's the one thing that keeps me from getting high," he said. And later, when I refused to give him the card, "If I die, it's your fault."

We got invited to Clark's wedding because when I was picking up my marriage license, I saw him at City Hall applying for his own. He'd decided on a quickie marriage before joining the Navy. It was a bad idea, but it's not polite to tell people when they're making disastrous choices. At his reception, LauraBeth and I were standing outside by the bar and looking at the trees (the wedding was at an arboretum, because a wedding has to happen someplace). We were doing what we try to do at most parties: quietly receding into the background. An older man stepped outside and fell to his knees, clutching his chest. He said, "It just hurts too much," before tumbling forward and groaning like he'd been shot. I thought I was watching him die. Before LauraBeth could check on him, his wife rushed outside and reassured us he had recently had shoulder surgery and his heart was fine. To die of a bad heart at a wedding would be too heavy-handed a metaphor. I flashed to a future version of myself, writhing on the ground in that same level of pain in front of strangers much younger than me, my heart failing while

I'm wearing a rented tux. I could imagine worse deaths, but that one ranked pretty low on the list.

Usually, we gave money as a gift, but for some reason we bought a wok off Clark's registry and had it shipped to his house. A couple months later, we received a thank you card from his wife that said, "We will love and cherish the fry pan always," and a month after that, they were divorced due to his bad habit of getting other women pregnant. I didn't hear from Clark again until after my third book was published two years later, when he sent me a direct message on social media asking me to Venmo him some money. He was really hurting for cash, he said. He wanted to get back into the studio to work on his rapping, he said. He sent two more messages, and I didn't respond, and that turned out to be the end of our friendship (he overdosed a month later, and now his widow logs on to his Facebook every day to post pictures of their children, sometimes crying, sometimes rapping along to the one song their dad posted on YouTube). Most stories don't end gracefully, no matter how much we try to convince ourselves they will.

I got a text in November 2008 from Diane, my high school friend from the driving classes. We'd both moved around the country in pursuit of graduate degrees, jobs, and relationships, but now and then we exchanged emails. Barack Obama had been elected President that evening. Her text said, "I cannot believe we are seeing history. I'm crying." I wouldn't hear from her again for a few more years, but eventually she would move back to the area and we would reconnect. As soon as we started talking, it felt like we'd never missed a minute together. Some of your friends are there for a very long time, and some of them seem like they were never there to begin with. There's not enough time for everyone.

2009

At the start of summer, we sold LauraBeth's childhood home. We learned how to do small repairs and stage a house and get the structure up to code, and the realtor told us it was best to sell before the market cratered even further. A year later, comparable houses in the neighborhood were selling for $20,000 less. The banks and the opioid crisis have blighted that town, like so many suburban neighborhoods. LauraBeth insisted she was not sad to have cut her final ties to her childhood. She didn't have time to be sad then because she had jobs to do. In crisis situations, she is skilled at focusing on the tasks that need to be completed. This is what makes her a good nurse (this is also why my mom liked her from the moment they met; good nurses respect one another instinctively). This is why I have designated her our captain in the event of a post-apocalyptic scenario, where we're scouring the countryside for life-saving supplies. I've floated the idea of a bomb shelter, or at least light doomsday prepping, but LauraBeth thinks this is insane, she says I worry too much about the apocalypse. She says if the apocalypse comes, we're better off letting it take us right away instead of forestalling the inevitable.

A month after selling the house, we drove down to DC for a Phillies game and carved out time to tour the White House. Around the perimeter, a variety of protest groups shouted over one another. A teenage boy stood against the fence reading his anti-war poetry in an act of symbolic defiance, and I tried to quell the cynical part of me that thinks symbols are stupid. The dominant protesters were a group of Southeast Asian people, their leader shouting into a megaphone. What we heard for sure: *President Obama! President Obama! Yes You Can! Yes You Can! Sri Lanka! Sri Lanka!* I couldn't decipher the last line. A Secret Service agent told us, "It's about fucking camels." He rolled his eyes. "The genocide of camels. What the hell are we supposed to do about that?" We laughed with him because it was absurd. But the word they were saying was *Tamils*. The chanting was about a genocide in Sri Lanka and nobody was listening. People were dying, and the Americans who might help them were ignorant and smug about it. I know I said symbols are stupid, but you have to admit, that's a pretty good one.

We took this road trip at the start of my summer break. LauraBeth did the driving, as she always does. I have never liked driving, and by the end of the year, I liked it even less. In October, I was crunched in the middle of a three-car pileup. I was physically fine but my car was totaled. The driver who caused the accident took off before the police arrived, I got sued by the driver in front, and the insurance company eventually settled the lawsuit (the insurance company's lawyer had a tattoo of a gecko on the arch of her foot; I wondered if every new employee was required to get one at orientation). I still can't drive near that bend on I-76, just past the South Street bridge, without tensing up and thinking about how, if any of a hundred variables had been slightly different, I could have been flung through my windshield or crushed beneath the weight of the car or who knows what. I find myself involuntarily tapping the brakes as I approach, trying to avoid an accident that happened 15 years ago.

I've been rear-ended three more times since then. The last time, the driver was a young guy who crouched behind his van, chain smoking and shaking and begging me not to call the police. He'd just gotten out of jail and was driving a work van for a new job. Getting the police involved might ruin, or at least derail, his life, But I was concerned about the damage and my insurance. A better person would have shaken his hand and let it go.

Two nights after the pile-up, LauraBeth and I test drove a new Civic and stopped at Boston Market, where we ate half chickens with two sides each and I convinced myself I needed a brand-new car, instead of a cheap used one. In my mind, buying a new car was a milestone in achieving adulthood. I financed an extra $15,000 at high interest mostly so I could feel like a grownup. Because I live close to work and can walk to the PATCO train into Philly, I drive fewer than 5,000 miles per year. Most of the time, the car is primarily storage for my ice scrapers and tire irons and Wawa receipts. The monthly bills over the next several years were a reminder that buying expensive objects doesn't make you a new person, it only depletes you.

I did experience one breakthrough around that time: for the first time in my adult life, I felt like I was good at my job. For five years prior to this, I had stood in front of my classrooms in a state of near-panic, ready to melt down the moment one element of my plan went awry. One otherwise unremarkable morning, I walked into the room, scanned the students' faces and thought: *I belong here, and I don't care anymore whether they think I'm cool.* To no longer worry about being cool, something I never had been, freed me of a burden I'd carried my whole life.

By a rough estimate, I have read over 21,000 student essays in my life, over 75,000 pages of freshman writing. Read enough of these papers in a row, and the language will lodge itself in your head forever. I can diagnose their problems within a few minutes: no argument, poor organization, poor source use, sloppy and imprecise language. Pick two of the above, and you've graded more than half of the essays.

Even the best student papers are a little boring. To subject yourself to them over and over again must damage your own ability to think critically. Over time, you will begin thinking about what happens in today's society, and how things have been a certain way since the dawn of mankind. You will begin sentences with, "With that being said," and wrap ideas up with "in conclusion, everyone nowadays has their own opinion." When I saw the Sri Lankan protesters at the White House, I imagined an essay beginning

"Throughout history people have said genocide is bad, but on the other hand some other people have said the opposite." I worry that I have become dull. I probably have, but it's not fair to pin it on my students.

In the depths of grading a massive stack of essays, I often think that we should just make a semester three weeks long, meet once to go over the rules, and then meet again so they can turn in their final papers. I try to remind myself most progress isn't linear, that not all growth is evident on the page. Some students improve dramatically and some show incremental improvement and some never do anything. Teaching is a long string of failures interrupted by occasional bursts of blinding clarity. Everyone in the room has aspirations, and my job is to remember how young and afraid and in need of support they are.

I have lost count of the number of times people—friends, family, strangers—have asked me when I am going to get a real job. I get summers off, and even during the academic year, I only have to go to campus two or three days a week. It is hard to quantify the impact I make by teaching writing. Culturally, there is a sense that college is a place everyone should go to, despite a generally held disdain for the work done by colleges. To many people in my life, my job is a hobby I practice when I want to vacation from lounging around the house. LauraBeth tells me I should defend myself when they disrespect me, but it's easier to move the conversation along, and I'm not going to change their minds anyway. I downplay the work because I feel guilty about having a job I actually enjoy, one that pays well and offers a sense of fulfilment. I feel guilty about getting paid to talk about books with autonomy while so many others are being destroyed by their work. Nothing seems fair if you think about it for long enough. I argue it's healthy to always remind myself how good I've got it, relative to most people, how tenuous it all is.

2010

It was December on Sanibel Island in Florida, and LauraBeth's older brother was getting married. This capped our last big wedding year. Her younger brother had gotten married in July, and my mom remarried in August. When she started dating her eventual husband, she was afraid to tell me and Kevin, afraid we would be angry at her, but we were both happy she had found the comfort of a new person in her life, that she'd had the strength to overcome her grief in the first place. When she called a few years later and told me "Bill asked me to marry him and I said yes" (the very specific phrasing she used every time she told someone), there was nothing to do but celebrate.

I used the occasion of my mom's wedding to hand sell three copies of my memoir, which had been published on Father's Day weekend. It sold about 2,500 copies before going out of print, which was about 50,000 fewer sales than I had hoped for. It's been so long since I worked on that book, the person who wrote it feels like a stranger. That year, I answered many questions like, "Aren't you too young to write a memoir?" and "What have you ever done?" I wrote a book, that's one thing I had done. It was never clear to me why that wasn't enough.

At the reception on Sanibel, there was a long line for beer and a shorter line for bourbon, so I went for the bourbon, and I went back for more bourbon, and so on, until suddenly I couldn't see straight and then I was crouching behind someone's rental car and vomiting in the parking lot. It was only 8 PM. My new sister-in-law told me later that she had been talking to me minutes before the vomiting and I had appeared perfectly fine. It concerns me that I've been able to hide it so often when I've been that drunk. If I were sloppier, or struggled with more severe hangovers, I would probably have renounced alcohol 15 years ago. It would have saved me so much money and time. Every detail from the remainder of the night is erased from my memory. When you're falling apart, it all happens in slow motion and then suddenly it speeds up beyond your control. I've been told people were worried I would fall in a ditch, or get hit by a car, or run afoul of a gator (signs posted around the resort warned about "nuisance gators," a euphemism I have come to love). LauraBeth left the wedding and tended to me while I vomited and cried on the bathroom floor. I woke up before sunrise, oozed out of bed, and wrote her an apologetic and self-flagellating note, which she read but never acknowledged. We did not discuss it and we did not fight, but I had ruined one of the most important days of her life. I was 28 and I was drinking so much at weddings that I threw up in the parking lot before anyone had even done the Cupid Shuffle.

For years, my behavior at that wedding—which was a personal, private shame that happened to have occurred publicly—was treated as a family joke. They all eventually stopped joking about it, maybe because they got tired of it, or maybe because I finally stopped laughing along with them. Maybe they ran out of new comments to make about it, and if you live long enough, you can outrun almost anything.

I have not vomited from drinking since that wedding. I have not made a drunken spectacle of myself again, the way I used to in grad school, when I often realized halfway through dinner that I was slurring my speech and kind classmates would ask me if I was okay getting home by myself. I don't get in fights or spill my beer on people or pass out in weird places, not anymore. I don't drive drunk (hard to count how many times I had convinced myself I was only a little buzzed and was just fine to drive). I am careful now. When we are in mixed company, I go to great pains never to be the drunkest person in the room. I monitor the levels of everyone's drinks and even if my beer is long empty, I will wait to refill until someone else does too, because it feels like they're giving me permission. One loophole there is to surround yourself with drunker people. Another loophole is to be the only person in the room. Careful and reckless are relative terms.

Sometimes LauraBeth and I will split a bottle of wine and talk about the desire to balance healthy living with our concerns about dying young like our parents. Still, we exercise several days a week and always take the stairs and limit our sugar intake and have begun cooking vegetarian meals most days, and we have not gone out for fast food in years. In most ways, we are leading healthy lives. I admit this may be an addict's brain talking, but there is an argument to be made that if I might die in my early 50s like my dad (and his dad), I am preserving myself for nothing. You don't need to hit me with the counterarguments here, I know them. I know.

Let me tell you: I am typing this and thinking about going downstairs to have a beer. It's Thursday. I have just finished the first week of a new semester. Without a drink the night is long and dull. With a drink, at least you can look forward to the next drink. Even thinking like this scares me a little bit, and I tell myself it's better to say it out loud than to pretend it's not true. I remind myself there are hundreds of good reasons not to open a beer today. Most days, I won't have a drink.

I imagine a large empty bottle in my office, an opening too small for me to fit through, so I have to disassemble myself and feed my parts one at a time through the neck and into the body, piling each piece of myself in there and waiting for someone to come in and reassemble me, as a better, pristine version, a beautiful ship with billowing sails, a collector's item to place over the mantle and display to visitors, to say: This used to be Tom, he didn't look like this when we found him, but he's been fully restored. Look how good he could have been.

2011

Six weeks after an emergency cholecystectomy for an inflamed gallbladder, LauraBeth was still in recovery as we embarked on an Alaskan cruise. She and I spent most evenings sipping on Maker's Mark by a window in the Schooner Lounge. I can't say for sure that I saw whales, but now and then in the distance, I saw splashes and blurs of activity that I decided must have been whales. Every morning I hoped to see a humpback or a grey swimming alongside our boat, to make eye contact with one and feel some magic bond form between us (I've read so many books about whales, it only seems fair that I get to be friends with one). Our drinks were delivered by a young Filipino man who spoke enough English to take orders and to refer to us as *honeymooners* every time he saw us. There were actual honeymooners on the boat—at least one couple, younger than us, a handsome young guy with the look of a mid-market meteorologist and his wife, who every day wore a different article of clothing bedazzled with the words *Mrs. Padilla*—but I suppose we still exuded an aura of young love, at least enough to have impressed this one waiter.

LauraBeth stood next to me on the deck the morning we navigated the Tracy Arm Fjord and paused to stare at the Sawyer Glacier. Because it is relatively easy for smaller cruise ships to access, thousands of people visit this glacier every year. Presented with an enormous wall of blue-tinted ice, you can't help but feel a sense of true awe. It looks like a chunk of another planet that dropped onto ours, like it's the property of a superior race. I closed my eyes and felt its presence hulking over me; the cold emanates from it and seeps into your skin. It throbs with a power that dwarfs everything you've ever done or cared about. Without warning, pieces started crumbling into the water. First the chunks were small, but then a block of ice the size of my house cracked and separated and plunged into the fjord, displacing enough water to rock our ship.

Researchers estimate the glacier has retreated 2.3 kilometers over the past 50 years, and with each year it becomes harder for cruisers to visit. Though nobody onboard the boat says it, the prodigious wastefulness of the cruise ship itself is partly responsible for the rising temperatures that are melting the glacier. Tourism on this scale is not ecologically tenable. The glacier was dying because of me and I was taking pictures of it. I wasn't quite as concerned about global warming then as I should have been. I thought of it as one of many problems our country should consider addressing. I believed my token efforts at recycling and turning off my lights during the day and reusing plastic bags would make a difference beyond making me feel better about my complicity. Now, as I read weekly stories about how global warming is an existential threat, not just to whales and caribou but to all human life, I understand that the key to survival isn't in individual choices but in a radical restructuring of society (but does thinking like this absolve me of making those changes still? Am I making excuses for not trying harder?). Now it all feels like it's too late, especially because the TV news will not even use the words "global warming" for fear of upsetting viewers, and some members of Congress are the dumbest, most venal people in American history. The planet is dying and most people are finally aware, but there is a President in America who says things about climate change like:

"One of the problems that a lot of people like myself—we have very high levels of intelligence, but we're not necessarily such believers. You look at our air and our water, and it's right now at a record clean. But when you look at China and you look at parts of Asia and when you look at South America, and when you look at many other places in this world, including Russia, including—just many other places—the air is incredibly dirty. And when you're talking about an atmosphere, oceans are very small. And it blows over and it sails over."

He's always the college freshman who hasn't done the homework but thinks he deserves an A just for showing up. When he speaks, it's like watching an especially dumb goat try to learn English on the spot. Like they put a suit on America's swollen liver and called it the President.

A few months after the cruise, we went with LauraBeth's brothers and their wives to a summer Beerfest at the Philadelphia Zoo. This was the last time I saw Coldilocks, the female polar bear who lived for 37 years in North Philadelphia. She swam past us, oblivious to the decline of her species, unaware that my sister-in-law had just told us she was pregnant, indifferent to all of it. We drank samples of 11 kinds of beer and wandered around looking at the animals, and I read all the plaques I'd read a hundred times in my life, all the same facts about sloth bears and orangutans and naked mole rats. I told everyone about the time I beat an orangutan in arm wrestling, one of my favorite achievements to brag about though it's not strictly true—the zoo used to have a machine where you could test your grip strength versus that of a variety of apes, and almost immediately after my triumph over the orangutan I changed the story to something that sounded more impressive— and anyway nobody believed me. Without busloads of children to compete with, I could get right up against the fences and imagine that the animals and I were old friends. I started a conversation with an especially attentive hippo, who was more of a listener than a talker. He wiggled his ears as I told him about the time the monorail crashed. I had never been drunk in a zoo before, and it was one of the hottest nights I have ever endured. By 10 PM, it was still over 100 degrees, and when we got back to our house, we dragged our mattress downstairs to sleep on the living room floor. With a window AC unit blasting and two fans pointed at us, we still sweated through the night. Our corgis lay on either side of the mattress, alert and confused.

I turned on the TV hoping for some good news about the weather. The lead story was about a boy who had thrown acid on the face of a girl who had refused to date him. When I google it now, I turn up numerous stories about women being doused in acid by angry young men, but I can't find the one from that night. When the weather came on, they told us it was hot, and only getting hotter. It would always be hotter forever, though they didn't say it then.

2012

When LauraBeth's brother showed up to my 30th birthday party with a video camera and told me to say something to his unborn child—she was due in three months—I said, "This is the last time you're ever going to see me." In my head, it sounded funny, but it's hard now to see how it even qualifies as a joke, and my delivery made it feel especially bleak (not feasible to count how many jokes in my life have failed to even register for others as jokes). Nobody laughed. I pretended I had to do something urgently in the kitchen so I could get away from the camera.

Back in college, I used to tell LauraBeth that I planned on being dead by the time I was 35. She didn't like me talking like that, but I thought joking about being dead made me seem introspective and thoughtful (I'd never read Nietzsche, but I aspired to be kind of guy who read Nietzsche). I didn't want to be deep so much as I wanted to be perceived by others as deep, and I often confused depression with depth.

I had been moping about this birthday since Christmas. I no longer wanted, or expected, to be dead at 35, but for the first time in my life my mortality felt real. The previous summer I had injured my back carrying a suitcase, and I had never felt older or more decrepit than that morning when I was in too much pain to brush my teeth, let alone to put on clothes or leave the house; LauraBeth had gently lowered me down into a rolling office chair and wheeled me around our Airbnb until I felt well enough to move on my own. I did not want to have a party, and I did not want gifts, and I did not want to talk about it (most years, I don't want any of these things anyway, and LauraBeth reminds me that it's not even about me, the birthday celebration is for everyone). I declared that my ideal birthday would be spent alone in the dark in the basement, maybe with one balloon. I was unpleasant company for months. Someone asked during dinner why I was so sad, and I resented that I was expected to talk about it. Every subsequent birthday, I will be asked if I'm feeling as depressed as I was on my 30th, and the answer is no, thankfully, but I also don't think I should have to justify having been sad. At some point you realize you are stuck inside this one flawed body, forever. Having a brain is one thing but having to house it inside a body is a whole new indignity.

After a few drinks I was more talkative and pleasant (this kind of positive reinforcement from alcohol causes me a whole different set of problems). I got a dartboard with a nice cabinet for the bar in my basement. I got a beautiful scrapbook from my aunt, who had spent weeks laboring over it. On the first page was a letter from Kevin that opened with a joke about how my mom had, characteristically, asked him four months in advance to write it, and ended like this:

> What I want to say is not that the things you've accomplished are admirable, because of course they are, but that they are yours and yours alone that I admire most. You've had and accepted help but you've done the greatest a person can do and what no one can help you with, you did what you thought was right and did it your best.

We opened up the good bourbon and passed it around. We ate prime rib—the butcher had cut 10 percent off the price when he heard it was my birthday—and I was surrounded by people who loved me. A fat corgi named Maggie slept under the table while we ate. I forget too often how much good there is in my life, because I'm so focused on finding new ways to complain about everything I don't have.

My mid-30s were the happiest and healthiest period of my life so far. My body was still in decent shape, and my mind worked as well as it ever had. I had more confidence navigating most social situations than I once did. I was better at my job than I had ever been, and I had more money than I did 10 years earlier. Sure, my hairline had begun receding and I'd reached the age at which I would be grotesque to sports broadcasters (if an athlete over 35 makes a big play, they act as if he's performed a miracle, as if a mummy has escaped from its tomb and executed a backflip), but overall, I grew to like the person I am. I almost never feel bad about being alive.

At 30, I couldn't have seen anything like contentment coming on. All I saw was 40, and then 50, and then maybe that would be it, like my father dead long before 60. It's possible I am well past the midpoint of my life. This is true of every living thing, and it becomes truer each day. Another friend from high school recently died of an overdose, and there have been close calls for several other friends: cancer and accidents and suicide attempts. Around my 30th birthday, I woke up some nights from dreams in which people from my past—friends and enemies, people who were enemies but thought they were friends—were walking past my coffin and looking down at me and mouthing their prayers while stripping off my clothes and writing messages on my body in magic marker, every inch of me covered in words I could never read because my eyes had been sewn shut. For most of this year, I felt worse than I had the day before, and then one day I didn't. I have a nice, safe life, and I have hardly done anything to deserve it. I don't know how it all works. I keep trying to figure out how one is supposed to handle that.

The day my niece was born, I was sitting along the banks of the Schuylkill River with LauraBeth's father and younger brother, watching her and her co-workers row to a last-place finish in a charity boat race as part of the Dad Vail Regatta, one of the biggest rowing events in the country. Her older brother was already at the hospital with his wife and newborn daughter. For months, LauraBeth had been training after work, and when people asked her why

116

she was doing it, she shrugged. It wasn't really fun, but it was something to do. A new way to challenge herself in her downtime (one attribute of hers I admire is that she's always trying to improve, always challenging herself in some way). I waited for her during some of her practices, sitting on a bench by the river and straining to read a book in the dark. They knew all along that they would lose, but they kept showing up anyway. Watching her group cross the finish line, I applauded, and I thought: *Isn't it nice to be alive?* None of it had ever felt possible, and yet here we were.

2013

There was the time when I had to leave my house during a party to buy orange juice—LauraBeth had invited her brothers and their families over for brunch—and I was gone for 15 minutes, but nobody noticed. We had all been standing on the deck and talking about how hot it was; it was August and in August you talk about how it is currently hot or will soon be hot again. Mosquitos—we talked about those too. The paper wasp nests clinging to the eaves of my house. My hatred of having to maintain my lawn. Our AC units in decline. Home ownership demands the endless discussion of banalities because it's the leaky pipe, not Mothra or King Kong, that will destroy your home. We were talking and LauraBeth pulled me aside and told me it was time for mimosas. When I went into the kitchen to mix them, I saw we didn't have one of the two necessary ingredients, so I left.

If I were writing fiction, this is the part where I—or rather a character very similar to me, with a name like Skip McMillian and a job as a freelance copy editor—would get behind the wheel and drive toward the Wawa and then experience a sudden change of heart at the traffic light. He, or rather I, would look at the full Wawa parking lot and then glance in the rearview and think of the futility of purchasing orange juice for birthday mimosas and then keep on driving. Skip would drive three towns away and knock on a mysterious door that he clearly knows but the reader does not, and the first chapter would end, leaving the reader in suspense. On the other side of the door could be a criminal associate, setting the stage for a classic mystery. It could be an unrequited love, the first stage of a romance. It could be a wizard. Most likely, if I wrote it, the door would be answered by his second, secret wife, and the book would be about Skip finding himself, or about running from responsibility, or the numbing effects of life in the suburbs, or a fear of death. To add some gravitas to the narrative, I, or rather Skip, would contract a terminal illness and have to decide whether he can ever return to the home and family he had so rashly abandoned. I'd have to add a child in there, or at least a pregnancy. If I got really lucky, I'd be able to stretch it to 70,000 words and sell it to a pretty good press for $10,000 and then get a couple authors to call it "penetrating" and "illuminating" and "deeply felt."

It's such a relief not to be writing fiction, not having to make all that shit up. Because I'm writing nonfiction, I can tell you: I parked at Wawa, next to the dry cleaner where the proprietor stands in the doorway all day smoking so that all the clothes she cleans come back smelling like cigarettes, and I bought the orange juice. At this Wawa, there are always long lines of rundown people who look like they're banned from at least one bar. Some of them live in the apartment complex next door that rents moldy efficiencies for $500 a month. Fred, my father-in-law, lived there near the end of his life, after years of unemployment and illnesses; his bed filled most of the room, and everything was coated in the kind of sadness that constricts your lungs.

There are small moments on my drives alone when I try to imagine my life as a different person and realize how limited my imagination is. What I come up with, most of the time, is something like: me, but 10 pounds lighter. Or: me, but with a sandwich. Maybe this means I'm basically content. Maybe it means I have so little ambition that I can't ever exceed my current level of achievement.

I paid for my orange juice and rushed home because it never even occurred to me to go somewhere else. LauraBeth is closer with her siblings than anybody I know, and yet I had the pressing feeling that she shouldn't be left alone with them. That my job at this brunch was to be present and act as a barrier in case someone began to act in some way annoying or burdensome. My job was to be helpful, in general, and not to get too drunk because when I get too drunk, I talk too much and I can tell she's disappointed in me. After a couple mimosas, everyone else stopped drinking, so I did too, though I wanted another drink. There was a whole day left, and I had no idea how to fill it.

LauraBeth likes brunch because she struggles with chronic fatigue. If we'd had her family over for dinner, she would have spent the whole day worrying about getting to bed too late. She would have convinced herself that staying up late one day would have a domino effect, and she would be on the verge of a spiral of anxiety that could ruin her whole week. She's a strong person, stronger than me, but I've told her I worry she may be one more trauma away from really losing it. Maybe we're all one trauma away from really losing it, and the line between lost and not is so thin and permeable that the only thing keeping most of us on the right side is the delusion that we belong there.

Here's the punchline of this story, I always forget the punchlines: nobody knew I was gone. I had left my own house, in my car, and driven a half mile away, and everyone had continued as if I had been there the whole time. It's not that I needed them to be waiting at the door with balloons and firecrackers. But I wondered how long I would have had to be gone before someone noticed. In the novel I did not write, would Skip (or rather I) have disappeared while the rest of the family continued living as if I (or rather Skip) had never existed in the first place? It's best not to think about some things for too long.

2014

We rented a house for a week in Cape May with LauraBeth's brothers and her father, Fred. We'd done this eight years earlier, after
LauraBeth and I had gotten engaged, and this time there was an
infant and his toddler sister who still did not like to acknowledge
his existence. There was a pregnancy. There was another adult
there, too—Fred's long-term girlfriend. Both of them had cancer.
Only when we were drunk at night and Fred was out of earshot did
we admit that we were worried he would die soon.

In the morning, LauraBeth and I lay in bed while her brother's
daughter stomped in the hallway outside our door, screaming for
her aunt. We ducked under the covers and tried to stay silent, hoping we'd locked the door. It was too early for all of this, and we
stayed in bed an extra 20 minutes just because we could. Coffee
was already brewing when we got downstairs. Toys and cups and
beach accessories scattered across every surface. The spiny ten-
drils of some kind of weed growing through the trim around the
kitchen window. A few spots on the kitchen floor felt soft enough
that if you jumped you could plummet through, and we all learned
to avoid them by day two. The nice thing about a vacation in a place
like Cape May—somewhere that you've seen plenty of times before
and that has few tourist attractions besides the beach—is you can
live an unstructured day. A slow breakfast. Coffee on the porch. A
lazy game of Scrabble. No pressure to go anywhere.

The big news that morning was that Robin Williams was dead.
Another reminder that the public persona reveals nothing about
one's inner life. The conversation at our table was the same as it was

at thousands of breakfast tables that morning: he always seemed so joyful, it's such a shame he couldn't get the help he needed, what were your favorite Robin Williams movies, and so on. I scrolled through Twitter for more information, but most of the people I followed were posting about the unrest in Ferguson. I had missed the story entirely up to that point. Michael Brown was killed on Saturday, when we were packing the car and driving into town and exploring the rental. The next two days I was mostly disconnected from media because I was at the beach and eating free samples of fudge and stocking the fridge with meat and beer and reading books on the porch. I had missed the story because I didn't have a specific need to be aware of the story, because my life is such that I can comfortably ignore racial injustice if I want to. Every week there's a new thinkpiece somewhere about how disconnecting is "self-care," but so many people can't afford to disconnect, don't have the option to not know. Self-care is one of those terms that used to have a specific meaning and now it's shorthand for doing whatever you want.

I watched the videos of the tear gas and the violence. I read all the predictable insane takes on it. A few months later, I saw a neighbor's car decorated with a bumper sticker that says, "Pants up, Don't loot," a parody of the sincere, desperate chant, "Hands up! Don't Shoot!" All bumper stickers are bad, but it seems to me that they keep getting worse.

Like many white Americans, I learned about the Black Lives Matter movement. I immediately saw people tweeting All Lives Matter and Blue Lives Matter, and thousands of jokes in attempts to siphon some attention off this protest movement. Now, nearly a decade later, about 10 percent of the houses in my mostly-white suburban neighborhood fly Blue Lives Matter flags of all varieties: the ones that are in grayscale except for the blue stripe, suggesting that the police aren't just good but are in fact better than us; the ones where the middle line is half red, due to the weird belief that liberals somehow represent a threat to firefighters; the especially bizarre ones that are all black and have a single blue line running through; and there's one house that has a flag with the outline of New Jersey, stars filling the North half, blue stripes filling the South. I cannot possibly interpret this display in any other way than the support for a rogue police state.

All day I was distracted and trying not to burden the family with my scattered thoughts about the videos of a city on fire, the victim blaming and police worship, besides which I was, as usual, worried about being too much of a downer, ruining everyone's nice week by forcing them to talk about depressing topics. I was observing an important historical moment, but also feeling outside it. The next decade would be marked by the regular appearance of police shooting videos, many of which looked like clear-cut cases of murder; they have become ubiquitous enough that even my students can rattle off the names of victims as if reciting baseball stats. Sometimes these are murders of children, though the apologists will insist they were especially large or intimidating children. It became easy around this time to feel hopeless. I read hundreds of articles about the issue, by which I mean I did nothing to ameliorate the problem. Feeling bad about it doesn't count as activism.

Ferguson has nothing to do with Robin Williams, but they happened at the same time. Ferguson has nothing to do with the pregnancies and births and the cancers, but they all were happening at the same time.

Fred had to leave midweek and go back to work. He was driving a courtesy shuttle for a car dealership, making barely enough money to survive, but at least they covered his health insurance. On the morning before he left, he sat on his bed with his granddaughter. She was going through a phase in which she fixated on identifying sadness. If someone read a book to her, she scanned the page for the saddest looking image and said, "Tree sad?" or "Cat sad?" or "Egg sad!" I relate to this habit on a fundamental level. That morning, she said, "Pop-pop sad" over and over, and he agreed. "Yes, I'm sad," he said, and they echoed each other for a few minutes. He was

123

60 and had cancer, but it's not the cancer that would eventually kill him. One day, a few years later, his son would find him dead on the floor of his apartment, cause unknown, though he had been in poor health for a long time, the effects of 30 years of severe obesity. We never vacationed with Fred again. The next time we all went to Cape May was in September 2019, to scatter LauraBeth's mother's ashes in the Atlantic, a task she and her brothers had been putting off for many years. We drove to the lighthouse and stood on the beach looking out at the sea and trying to remember all of this, hoping it means something more in the end.

2015

Winter had been colder and more ruthless than usual, and our deck was covered in ice. Daisy, a senior beagle-basset mix who we adopted in the summer, took one step onto the ice and the sound of it cracking beneath her paw sent her scurrying back to the safety of her bed on the opposite end of the house. I yelled at her and was immediately flooded with shame. She was so afraid, had been abused for most of her life. We didn't know much about her history, but the vet had noted extensive damage to her teeth from years of trying to chew her way out of a cage. Sometimes if I reached out too quickly to pet her, she sprawled to the floor and flattened herself as if I was about to hit her. For the first three months after we adopted her, she howled so intensely on walks that you could hear her from a mile away. Despite all the trauma she'd endured, she was, and remains, the gentlest dog I have ever met. Unless she was sleeping, she never stopped wagging her tail. During the day, she slept in the sun in our bay window, and our neighbors told us they loved seeing her at her post, the world's worst security guard. When we came home, she stood creakily and howled one time, a sound I would come to miss very much after her death. The neighbor children swarmed her and petted her in eerie silence any time we were outside. Their parents shook their heads in pity and said we were good people for giving her a second chance at life. We allowed ourselves sometimes to feel smug about our choice to adopt a senior dog, rather than paying a breeder for an expensive puppy. Though we were (are) sometimes caricatures of suburban liberals with advanced degrees, I try to convince myself that not all my personal choices have been manipulated by whichever corporations own all my personal data. I insist still that we got the dog because we thought it was the right choice (though maybe we do buy the organic cage-free eggs because we've been fooled).

In the early days, Daisy was petrified of entering the kitchen. She stopped in the doorway, her body trembling, tail between her legs. If I tried to force her through the doorway, she ran and hid in the far corner of the living room. I spent weeks training her to enter the room, crouching and giving her a Cheerio for each tentative step she took. Some days we only made it five steps before she retreated. Some days we made it all the way through in a few minutes and I felt more pride than I ever had in any professional achievement.

After the cracking ice scared her, I needed to retrain her to trust this same route. It was my fault we had a new dog—after the corgis both died, LauraBeth had grown accustomed to the quiet and the lack of obligation, the freedom to come and go as we pleased, but I was lonely in the summer and had gotten into the habit of checking Petfinder's listings every day—and so it was my responsibility to teach the dog once again how to trust the ground beneath her feet. It took another week and a few hundred more Cheerios, but soon, she was able to go outside on her own. This process is arguably the purest act of love I have ever performed.

By summer, our yard was overrun with wildlife. At least 13 species of bird. Chipmunks. Gophers. Rabbits and squirrels and the occasional raccoon. Some mornings, a scowling, preening flock of wild turkeys. Surely there were mice probing for entry points into the house. None of them feared our pitiful, harmless dog, who wagged her tail as she strolled right past a nesting bunny, the only beagle in history completely uninterested in chasing things. By this point, we had rearranged much of our life around her quirks and her special needs. Some obvious ways—if she entered the kitchen, we froze, afraid to trigger another panic attack—and some more subtle—I sometimes left the house through the back door so she wouldn't notice that I was gone and get upset.

Because the animals had free rein over our yard, they often triggered the motion lights on our deck at night. The dog did not care because she never knew. Sometimes when I saw the lights flash on, then off, I listened for the creaking of the deck. And I had to determine: is this a curious raccoon or an intruder? If it's an intruder, is he alone? Is he going to break through the sliding glass door? Is he hoping for an easy score, or is this the last night of my life?

On the worst of these nights, when my paranoia was out of control, I crept toward the back door, looking for a weapon. Sometimes a hammer or crowbar or some other tool I'd left out for too many days. Most often, a Santoku knife, the one we used for dicing onions and peppers and carrots. I lay in wait in the dark, listening for any sign of danger. Would I use this knife to kill a man? What if he were assaulting my wife? I told myself it would be easy, that anyone can cross that line in the right circumstances. A number of friends and family members have been buying guns the past few years; they say it's a sad necessity, they shake their head at the situation that has forced them into gun ownership, but they also openly fantasize about how they will put three quick bullets into the chest of a home intruder the first chance they get. Thousands of innocent people get killed because someone in a safe neighborhood was daydreaming about being John Wick. My younger brother-in-law and his wife told us that they had considered getting a gun for protection, but the act of firing one at the range had been a reality check. It was so much louder and more frightening than they'd expected. Now they keep a baseball bat in the bedroom, just in case.

I'm intensely opposed to guns as a concept, think of gun culture as crippling to a functional democracy, view fervent Second Amendment people as a cruel and stupid and selfish constituency, but of course I have considered owning a gun. In these moments, while lurking in the kitchen trying to decide if I was about to fight for my life, I thought it would be extraordinarily satisfying to behave like an Elmore Leonard protagonist and come out firing (though most Elmore Leonard characters eventually get shot themselves, a fact I sometimes forget). Like a homesteader out there protecting his property from bandits. My real worry about owning a gun is that I would someday find a reason to use it.

Nothing was on the deck. It's always nothing, until the one time when it's not. I put the knife away and checked on the dog, who was curled into a tight ball on her bed and snoring. LauraBeth and I could both have been murdered and Daisy would never have known. I think at times I am trying to manufacture more drama because then at least it would give me something to talk about. That lingering adolescent part of my brain says at least then I could start writing essays *about* something. I tell my students all the time that memoir has nothing to do with major incidents, that it's about keen insights and vivid details and so on, but I'm always the last one to listen to my own advice. The dog isn't even the point. The imagined danger isn't even the point.

2016

From Cadillac Mountain in Acadia National Park, you can be the first person in America to see the sun rise. The morning of our anniversary, the sun was forecast to rise at 5:40 AM, so we woke up at 4:30, and drove from our bed and breakfast up the mountain. The line was longer and worse than we'd expected, and each successive minute the other drivers became more frantic. People pulled wild U-turns on narrow park roads. They drove on the grass, past signs imploring people not to endanger wildlife or ruin the habitat. Passengers leaped out of moving cars and ran toward the front of the line.

We parked and we hustled, and for the next five minutes we watched in silence as the sun appeared over the horizon. I took a few pictures, and most of them turned out blurry because I have never learned how to use my camera correctly. There were a few hundred people and everyone was pointing their phones at the sun. Do I need to describe the sunlight for you? It gets photographed so many times for so many reasons and it never diminishes in brilliance. The whole reason we're alive, a goddamn ball of gas so far away we couldn't travel to it in 10 lifetimes. None of it should be possible. But, man, the colors. You're going to have to take my word for it.

Every year we go on vacation to some new place, but we always end up at the nearest body of water. We end up standing together at dusk or dawn or both, looking up at the sun rising or setting and thinking about nothing. Not much is perfect, but this is.

By the time the whole sun was visible, half the crowd had already returned to their cars and begun streaming down the mountain.

We've traveled enough to know this is how it goes: people shove their way to the front of the line to see the famous attraction and they've already turned their back before the image has processed on their phone. The picture is the proof. It's the validation.

Soon, we had the park to ourselves. We drove around the perimeter stopping at scenic vistas, periodically reminding one another that we were fortunate to be here, to have the time and money and physical ability to travel wherever we want. We paused at Thunder Hole, an inlet famous for its acoustic properties that amplify the sound of the incoming waves. It was low tide, so not too thunderous, but I basically got the point. I assume it's the same at high tide, but louder.

We got back to the B&B in time for breakfast at the communal table, where one guy was talking about his finance job in New York as if anybody but New York finance people could possibly care. He described, in grueling detail, all the suits he owned and what colors they were. Another guest complained about her Mexican maid, who she didn't trust to be alone in the house. The B&B host talked incessantly about how much he hated Hillary Clinton; on his Facebook page, I found dozens of posts where he alternated between calling her Killary and Shrillary, and a few that suggested he believed in the lunatic Pizzagate conspiracy. There was broad agreement at the table that we needed a border wall and we needed it now. It had been an exhausting year, and the election was still two months away. All this nonsense was supposed to end in November that year, but it all would keep going (forever; it would keep going forever). LauraBeth and I left the table to take a nap, but I couldn't sleep because I was so agitated by the conversation. They say travel is broadening, but that's not true for everyone. A lot of people are assholes before they leave town and they're assholes when they get back. I don't know what category I fall into, but I swear I'm trying my best.

2017

Our flight landed too early at Charles de Gaulle for us to get into our Airbnb, so we stood on the corner next to the Sully-Morland Métro stop, leaning on our suitcases at dawn and trying to look like we belonged there. I'm comfortable in cities generally, but we were both groggy and LauraBeth spoke only rudimentary French. Neither of us can sleep on planes, no matter what we try; this time, we'd both bought $40 neck pillows with adjustable arms for cradling our heads, but when I wrapped it around my neck all I could think about was that I was a man using a $40 travel pillow. The noise canceling headphones couldn't cancel all the noise and people were constantly in motion; sleep was not possible. On the flight, I watched *Moonlight* and tried to read *The Brothers Karamazov*, but felt claustrophobic among all those blustery Russians pontificating about the existence of God while strangers brushed their asses against my shoulder on their way to the bathroom. High art doesn't belong in economy class. We had euthanized our dog Daisy only 24 hours earlier, and we were disoriented beyond any function. Our only goal was to be ignored by strangers until we could get into a bed. The city was still waking up, so for long stretches, nobody passed us at all.

I called the Airbnb caretaker, a Croatian woman who spoke some French and less English. She said something that sounded like she was coming to unlock the door soon. In America, I would have passed the time scrolling through my phone, but without an international data plan, my only option was to look at the world. LauraBeth and I talked about Daisy, the poor old beagle-basset mix who had stopped eating and drinking for most of a week and had begun confining herself to the darkest corner of our bedroom. The vet said she could run a battery of tests, but at Daisy's advanced age, it seemed cruel to subject her to more suffering. She gave us a rubric for determining when it's humane to euthanize: list the six activities she most loved to do, and if she was only doing half of them (or less), then we could be pretty confident her quality of life was poor. I'm not sure whether I even have six distinct activities I like to do (recently, I traveled to another university to speak to some classes, and afterward the faculty took me out to dinner; the Dean of Arts and Sciences asked me how I fill my spare time and I told him "I watch a lot of sports," to which he replied, "Okay, but what do you like to *do?*"). It's a calculation I now make often, trying to determine if activities I'm engaged in would make my list of six, if I could live without them, if they are simply a waste of time. We kept reassuring ourselves that we had made the right choice. You have to do that after you put a dog down because the guilt never goes away.

When we finally got into our room, I connected to the Wi-Fi to email my mom. She's always anxious when we're traveling and was especially concerned about us going to Europe in the wake of recent terrorist attacks. There's a chance that if you travel to any place in the world, a terrorist could kill you. There's a chance that either of us could be shot at our jobs, or in the mall, or at the grocery store. There's a chance my neighbor could be stockpiling military-grade weapons and waiting to ambush everyone at next weekend's farmer's market. I struggle sometimes to shut down that voice in my head, the one that says the only safe move is to never go anywhere, because if you go somewhere (anywhere), you might die.

After reassuring my mom that we were still alive and relatively well, I checked the news. Overnight, torch-wielding white suprem-acists had marched in Charlottesville chanting "You will not replace us." In the aftermath, the president had been personally aggrieved at having to declare that Nazi marches are bad. He's one of the least subtle men in history, and so it was easy to see that on some level, he thought Heather Heyer deserved to have been killed (he has since repeatedly expressed regret at having criticized the white supremacists, who, it goes without saying, love him because of his racism). I was too tired to process all this information. I had never held out hope for this president to be anything other than an historic disgrace, but I had also never imagined the specific details with which the disgrace would unfold. Everyone at home had been asking if we felt safe flying to France and meanwhile in the U.S., racist gangs were murdering people in the middle of an idyllic little college town.

I had been to Charlottesville that March to promote my novel. For three months in 2017, I traveled to literary events and my publisher paid for it, which briefly made me feel very important, even when few people turned up to my events. In Boston, we got three guests and made no sales because the books were never delivered to the store. Afterward, I ordered a $23 bourbon at the hotel bar and lost my credit card. In Charlottesville, I sold four books and ate a great burger and had an afternoon beer before boarding my bus home. I was on the bus when LauraBeth called to tell me her father had died, leaving my mom as the only living parent between us. I was four hours away and useless to her. I had edits due on a new book and had to email the editor to explain that I could not possibly hit my deadline.

It was a busy and often unhappy year. In the backdrop of all of it were the protests. In January, my promotional event in Vermont had been a success, but when I landed at home, the airport was overrun with people protesting the Muslim ban. I heard a police officer telling his partner he wished someone "would just knock all these faggots out," and I thought it would be easier to like the police if they didn't act so much like cops all the time.

It would have been beautiful if flying across the ocean had allowed us to forget it all. That's what travel was like before the internet; you packed some bags and flew a couple hundred miles away and home did not exist. At least we got to sleep in a different bed and eat different foods. Our trip in summary: learning the Métro & climbing lots of stairs & walking & taking pictures & gargoyles & wine carafes & outdoor cafes & crêpes & a downpour at Versailles & so much cheese. We left the flat early every morning because our toilet had broken and would not flush, so we had to find cafés with public toilets. Over breakfast, I read the terrible news to LauraBeth, who wished I would stop reading the news. The Eiffel Tower was a grimy and unpleasant spectacle. Everywhere, there were police and military carrying assault rifles. I never felt unsafe, not because of the security but because it would have been so pointless to die on vacation (I keep thinking one's death has to mean something, I keep reminding myself it almost never does).

We celebrated our 10th anniversary in a bistro across the street from our flat. Sometimes while we're eating together, I'll think about how miraculous it is that we still have new things to talk about. The incredible fortune of finding someone who can tolerate you for so long! While we ate, the president tweeted in defense of Confederate monuments, and about how important it is to protect our borders. I thought, for the first time in my life, what if we don't go back there? Who will even notice?

2018

I spent most of 2018 not writing, filling my days by obsessing over social media and the news in ways that have rotted my brain. If I typed a few good sentences, I rewarded myself by clicking ALT+TAB over to Chrome, so I could check Twitter, where I read about:

- Somebody's especially fat cat
- YouTube's algorithms accidentally building a massive network of pedophiles by linking them to videos of young girls
- Several more cats, piles of cats
- People posting the distracted boyfriend meme, every day, endlessly

Over the previous two years, I had lost faith in the project of fiction. I published two novels in that time, and there were interviews and reviews in all the good places, but almost nobody has bought or read the books. The loss of faith was not just about sales or prestige; it was about living in a decaying world in which I feel silly sitting down and writing a made-up story. All I could think is that what I'm doing is pointless, that nobody could ever care what happens to these fake people. It felt like something a child would do.

Maybe you're thinking that fiction is an escape, and escape has real value. The act of creation helps to make the world more beautiful and livable. Some of the greatest artworks in history were produced at times of unfathomable strife and fear. Fiction can illuminate reality in ways nonfiction cannot.

I get it. I do.

Most days, I prefer a novel or some kind of genre film to yet another documentary about a humanitarian crisis that I cannot even begin to comprehend. I don't mean to degrade all novels, just my own. Writing these essays, I'm finding some solace in shrinking the world around me and fortifying myself. I am trying to order my life in such a way that I can validate my existence. Clicking back to Twitter, I saw:

- Another conservative pundit writing another disingenuous argument about free speech on campus
- One of my friends had bought a wig
- A literary organization was selling sassy tote bags
- An acquaintance had published a story, which I clicked and opened in a new tab that I hoped I would eventually read, before the end of the year

For much of this year, I felt, for the first time in my life, that I was perpetually on the verge of tears. Showing a documentary to my students, a movie I had at that point seen nine times, I had to look away when an adorable eight-year-old sang about how she was going to make it to the top; she lived in the projects in New York City and statistics tell us she is probably not going to make it, not even to the middle, and I felt overwhelmed by all of it. I don't even like sneezing in front of my class—it reminds them I have a body—so there's no way I could abide crying there. At night, I tried watching a nature documentary, and when a prehistoric-looking bird called a shoebill abandoned one of its two chicks, the little one shrieking in panic as its mother and brother strode away, I cried in the darkness of my living room. I'd never even heard of shoebills, but I watch nature shows specifically so they can manipulate me emotionally. I used to sit in my dorm room and watch *Faces of Death*. Used to play the Budd Dwyer suicide video for anyone who stopped by. Watched and rewatched a friend's VHS collection of the best hockey fights. Now I fast forward through bloody fight scenes in movies. I turn away when an athlete gets injured.

It's a sign of maturity that I don't find other people's pain entertaining anymore. But there's something else happening too, something more insidious and permanent and heavier.

For much of this year, our house was a sad house, despite our best efforts. The day after Thanksgiving, one of LauraBeth's closest friends was visiting. After a few cocktails, he told her, "You really need to go to therapy." She laughed and brushed it off, the same way her father used to turn it into a joke when we said he needed to lose weight and be more active. When she went to the bathroom, her friend said, "Seriously, she needs to go to therapy." I know, I said. Later, I recounted this conversation for her. I know, she said. For real, I said. I know, she said.

Back on Twitter I saw:

- A friend promoting her book
- A humpback whale's stomach was full of plastic
- The *Dilbert* guy was shirtless and flexing again
- A one-panel comic about a sad dinosaur

I almost forgot to mention we got another new dog. After we euthanized Daisy, LauraBeth was once again enjoying her freedom from the responsibility of keeping another mammal alive. She'd been enrolled part-time in a graduate program for Public Health— people kept asking: "What are you going to do with a Public Health degree?" Her answer, "I just want to learn," which did not seem to satisfy, so they asked if she would get a raise, and she said no, so then they asked the first question again. Because she was so busy with school, she had told me, explicitly, that she wanted to graduate before we got another dog. But I was bored and wanted to feel useful. I'd tried building a feral cat shelter in the back yard, but no cats ever sheltered there, and I trashed it when I saw a portly raccoon strutting through the yard as if she was considering moving in. For a month, I fed the birds, and if you accept the premise that it's better for the world to have more fed birds than unfed birds, it was a good thing to do, but it did not make me feel less lonely. When we'd moved into our first house together, I'd floated the idea of hanging a bird feeder from the tree in the corner of our yard, and my father-in-law shot me a grave look and warned that a bird feeder is a major responsibility. "You don't want them to rely on you unless you're going to take care of it every day." The birds, he said, would be worse off with an inconsistently maintained feeder than with no feeder at all. Viewed through this lens, my clumsy efforts at benevolence were another selfish act.

The Homeward Bound Pet Adoption Center has a program that lets you "rent" a dog, sort of a dog library, where you give them your contact information, and then hang out with a dog for the next few hours. On summer break, I rented a pit bull mix named Taco. It was a hot day and I didn't know what to do with him after our walk. It was like being on a first date. We drove around for a while with the air conditioning blasting, and we listened to a basketball podcast (he didn't express much interest in the Knicks or the Jazz but I felt like he perked his ears up when the host talked about the Bulls, some sort of mammalian kinship).

For two weeks, I showed pictures of Taco to friends and family, and then I saw on the shelter's Facebook page that he had been adopted. The new owner posted a video of him sleeping on a couch and twitching. "My son is having a dream!" the owner said. I am telling you, I cried more in that year than I had in the previous three decades combined.

The dog we subsequently adopted was a black and white pit bull named Gus, who had a head the size of a watermelon and in the summer got a little strip of sunburn on the tip of his nose. He was abandoned by his previous owners, so his separation anxiety was severe enough that we started him on 20 mg of Prozac. The meds meant I could leave the house without him leaping onto tables and breaking our lamps, though he might still pee on our dining room floor. He brought disorder to the house. He created messes and he wanted to wake up by 7 AM no matter what. In the best case scenario, he would have been a burden on us for at least five more years, but I felt better having another living creature nearby. As it turned out, he would die suddenly from a ruptured spleen only two years later, now the bearer not of disorder but of misery. I'd made my wife's life worse by bringing him home (I like to think of myself as a good husband, but doesn't everyone?). I wanted her to go to therapy partly because I was afraid if she didn't, she wouldn't have anyone to talk to about her frustrations with me. I'm afraid of being alone. That's what it's always been about.

2019

This was the summer we finally had wills drafted and met with a financial advisor to develop something called a Life Goals Plan. Steve, the advisor, had a penchant for repeating himself five or six times in a row, which reminded me of my deceased father-in-law and was the main reason I had booked our first meeting with him; I trusted he would patiently, and gently, explain the vagaries of finances to us. We are both smart people who do not understand anything about how money works, though I assure you we have tried. We met with Steve several times to discuss our current savings, our aspirations, our specific financial goals, and the obstacles we might face. His office was a single sparsely decorated unit in a nondescript complex in Cherry Hill, New Jersey, a town that, like many in South Jersey, has its charms but is mostly numbered highways connecting strip malls. He is married, and I hope some days he gets to go home for lunch with his wife, or that they talk on the phone or something. On the windowsill he displayed a Rookie of the Year trophy from the Toastmasters. The detail I remember most clearly about him was that instead of saying, "What ends up happening," he would say, "What lands up happening." This is a phrase he managed to use often enough that it has since infected both of our speech patterns.

Steve asked us how long we expect to live, so he could walk us through what would land up happening. Our options were 95, 93, or 91 years. We asked if he could plan for something closer to, say, 65, which would have us outliving three of our four parents. This was not a joke, but he laughed because people don't know how to respond when you talk about death like this. He emphasized that his job is to consider all contingencies, so by planning for the longest possible life, he can give us the best chance at success. Eventually, he ran a scenario in which LauraBeth lived to 93 and I lived to 91. On a line graph showing our projected earnings and expenditures over the remainder of our lives—factoring in inflation, this program projected more than a million dollars in healthcare costs in our retirement years, a number no reasonable person can expect to be able to pay—we were presented the most optimistic version of our future that a computer could generate. In the year 2073, suddenly the expenses were cut in half. *Tom's plan ends*, an annotation said, euphemistically. *LauraBeth's plan continues*.

At the end of our meeting, Steve gave us a 100-page binder filled with dozens of charts and graphs, each a different permutation of our possible futures. Looking at the graphs, I tried to comprehend the dire implications of every peak and valley. I understand that, to nearly every being on the planet, I either don't exist or, if I do, I am a single data point in an infinitely sprawling graph, bouncing along until the algorithm determines my value has been reduced to zero. For most of my life, I would have clung to this notion and thought it constituted a kind of wisdom, proof of the general pointlessness of existence. I would have used it as an excuse to justify my nihilism, to shrug and laugh and pretend nothing matters. There are times when thinking like this feels like honesty, but that's a delusion that only makes you sicker. On days when I feel that familiar despair sinking deep into my bones, I try to turn away from the horizon and instead lower the microscope onto the smallest, least consequential aspects of my life. I push back on that voice that tells me I'm selfish for needing to look away and disengage for a minute. I try to shut out the inevitability of collapse and the crushing weight of the world's indifference and remember the individual moments I get to live: the warmth of my wife in bed next to me on a Saturday morning; the smell of her perfume on the pillow when I wake up without her; the relentless chatter of the sparrows in the trees in my backyard; a hot sandwich straight out of the toaster oven with melted cheese oozing off the edges and crusting onto the sides; my dog snoring on the couch next to me as I read a good book, the cushions vibrating slightly with each inhale; the sun rising over the woods, shining through the trees and into my office as I type something that feels like it has a chance to be pretty good; the freedom of a summer weekday where I am accountable to nobody in the world except my wife and my dog, free to take a walk or watch a movie or do nothing at all; the last cool fall night when I sit on my deck with a fire crackling and a cold beer and a book I am holding but not really reading while John Prine plays on the speakers; the rare and perfect moments when we are all out to dinner as a family and everything clicks into place, nobody dealing with any drama or pain, nobody annoying anybody else, just a family together and laughing at the same old jokes and emptying a carafe of wine and ordering another round of appetizers and feeling invincible.

I know all the ways I'm supposed to feel bad. I think about them most of the time. But for fleeting moments, I forget them all, and I am a person who is alive and who has people who love him. That's pretty good, all things considered. I sit at my desk and close my eyes and breathe it all in and I try to remember.

2020

We moved into a new house in the summer, and I hope it's the last move we ever make. Our house went up for sale the day before the Governor announced the pandemic stay-at-home order, but the real estate industry was one of the first, and nimblest, in inventing loopholes and workarounds. When prospective buyers visited the house, my dog Gus and I sat on a bench at a public park that was flooded with people desperate to get out of their homes. Many wore masks. They all cut wide berths around us; we were sharing the same space, but still isolated. After the prospective buyers left, I opened all the windows and sprayed every surface with Lysol. I worried that if I breathed too deeply, I would inhale the disease and be dead within the week.

The house we bought is less than half the size of the one we sold. This was not primarily a financial play—we wanted to downsize, the old house over 2,600 square feet just for the two of us, three whole rooms we never used for anything besides storing junk, though when we'd moved in, we thought Fred might need to live with us as he aged and declined, or that my mom, before she married, might need an in-law suite, not to mention that for a few years we were babysitting our young niece at least one weekend a month. Because we were downsizing, we netted a healthy profit on the dual transactions. For the first time in our lives as homeowners, we had money to spend, not just chasing one repair to the next, but making actual improvements to the house. I hired someone to build a custom shed in the corner of the yard. I hired a landscaper to plant 15 shrubs and an October Glory Maple back there too. After the work was done, he said, "Please promise me you will keep these plants watered." He folded his hands in prayer. "Every day, I go to people's houses and have to remind them these are *living things*. They don't just *jump into a hole* and sit there like rocks." I was glad to have something to do in the mornings, standing outside with the hose for a half hour while I listened to a podcast, every episode of every show back then beginning with apologies from the hosts, who weren't sure if it was okay or even advisable to still be recording. Later, I bought a sprinkler and watched streams of water flip gymnastically in high arcs across my lawn. I stood beneath the stream like a child and let it soak through my shirt.

Besides being smaller, our new house has a bedroom on the first floor, which we are prepared to use in the future should one or both of us become incapable of climbing stairs. Some friends have responded to this plan with wide-eyed horror. To these friends, who still want to think of themselves as young and vibrant, it sounds like pessimism, maybe even like giving up. But to me it's the optimistic view that we will grow old enough to become decrepit in this house. To outlive our parents by so long that we can even have those years of decline to worry about.

During our home inspection, we entered the attached garage and saw a cluster of trash cans and boxes stacked against the wall. "One way to know something's wrong," the inspector said, "Is when there's a bunch of shit all piled in the same spot." Behind the pile of shit was evidence of a persistent leak; the inspector determined the garage had been built incorrectly, below the soil line, so that the drywall and studs themselves were underground. Early in the pandemic everyone started hiring contractors to fix everything, so our usual handyman was booked out nine months in advance. Kevin, who is significantly handier than I am, who knows the names *and* functions of any number of tools, helped me with a variety of small projects, including addressing the live wires the previous owners had left behind in the middle of the yard when they moved their hot tub out. He and I agreed that I should call in a professional for structural work, so I eventually hired a guy named Paul, whose main qualification was that he called me back. I don't think he had a drug problem, but sometimes I wonder how his behavior would have differed if he did. He had a tendency to do about 90 minutes of work, then text me from the next room asking me to come outside. He had to leave for some vaguely defined reason, but could I pay him in cash for the work he'd completed that day? Over a period of six weeks, I gave him small amounts of cash—once as little as 20 bucks—on 13 separate occasions. The thing is, every contractor is kind of weird. It would be more noteworthy if he'd shown up on time every day and finished the job within a week.

My office is an 8x12 box carved into the east-facing side of our attic, comfortable enough but nothing special. It sits atop the garage, which I didn't realize until I was upstairs working on a failed novel and felt every thump of the hammer and vibration of the reciprocating saw. Paul was a very tall man, and now and then he banged his head on the support braces he'd built, and then I heard a blur of profanity through my floor. One afternoon, he texted, "Come look at this," a message one never wants to receive from a contractor. He pointed at the open wall. Three of the studs were so rotted that they were no longer connected to the framing at the bottom. "I don't know how this works," he said. "Somehow, your roof has been holding the walls up."

After we looked at the dysfunctional wall a while, he said something about leaving to take his kid to the hospital. I mentioned that LauraBeth was a nurse at that same hospital, and he grabbed my hand. He shook it and maintained intense eye contact: "When your wife gets home, I want you to tell her she is a hero, and I thank her for her service." This was during that brief window when people talked about nurses like they were troops. I never felt especially comfortable with it—and never thought it was sincere—but it was better than what would happen a few months later when maniacs across the country would begin threatening doctors and nurses who wanted to help them stay alive.

Paul returned the next day and nearly finished the job. In his words, there were about 40 minutes of work left to do. He didn't explain why it would be easier for him to leave than to hang around for another 40 minutes. He vowed to return very soon, which obviously he never did.

During this time I was watching every video and livestream I could find of the protests over George Floyd's murder. I cheered the protesters, cursed the police, and posted my outrage on Twitter, but I never dared to get within a mile of the action. I used Covid as an excuse not to go to Center City and march on the Ben Franklin Bridge alongside the others, but the real excuse is that I was afraid of being shot with rubber bullets. Or worse. I gave money to restorative justice organizations because I did not have the courage to use my body. I don't know if the donations helped anything. I have money now, more than I ever thought I might, and it often seems like an accident. The arbitrariness of my own comfort gnaws at me. Not enough to make me give it up.

When I work in my office, I am grateful for functional walls, for floors and ceilings that work the way they're supposed to work. I'm grateful for my healthy lungs and for my job that allows me to stay isolated for weeks at a time if necessary. I'm grateful to own a home in a desirable neighborhood, where the value has increased exponentially through no doing of my own. The view out my window is of the vinyl siding on my neighbor's house. There is no magic in this place, but I'm not one of those writers who gets precious about writing spaces. There's room enough for a desk and a chair and scattered piles of books. I have since gotten very close to adding a few decorations to the wall. It's more than anyone reasonably needs, even if it's not romantic. There were days when I thought I'd never have any of it. There are many days still when I know I don't deserve it.

2021

After years of talking about volunteering in the community, LauraBeth and I signed up to join a new organization that had been formed during the summer of 2020 by a group of restless and angry parents who wanted, like so many of us, to do *something* about *something*. They were planning a Pride parade and a full weekend of related events, the first in the history of our town. A few weeks after signing up, we sat on the couch close enough to each other so we could both appear on the little Zoom window during our introductory meeting. About 20 other people were logged on. The organizers were still figuring out what they even wanted to do, let alone how to do it; after two hours, we signed off, not entirely sure what was going to happen next or what they needed from us. Besides a brief introduction, neither of us spoke.

A correction: of course we spoke, but to each other, with the mic muted, muttering about people who proposed ridiculous ideas or made endless rambling comments or got up more than once to refill their wine. We both had wine too, but it was off-screen, less uncouth. Despite having lived in this town for a decade—and a nearby town for five years before that—we knew almost nobody. A few neighbors who recognize me from my daily dog walks (we have another new dog, a pit bull mix named Teddy Bagel, who has a complex series of allergies and chronic ear infections but is nonetheless the easiest dog we've ever owned). Two friends from college. A handful of people who were friends of those friends but somehow never seemed to remember any of the numerous times we'd met them, and so we were always reintroducing ourselves. We don't have kids, is the main issue. Outside of the workplace, that's how adults meet other adults: they stand on the sideline of a youth softball game and chitchat, and they hope their kid ends up becoming friends with some of the kids whose parents aren't insane. They go to PTA meetings and school plays and birthday parties and gradually get to know all manner of people.

It wouldn't be strictly true to say we were lonely, but the last year had crystallized how isolated we'd been. I had the illusion of friendships with hundreds of people because I was online all day, and because I was posting weekly episodes of my podcast, which could almost feel like I was maintaining a dialogue with all these acquaintances. But mostly I was, I am, an anonymous man in a densely populated suburb. Outside of my mom, Kevin, and Laura-Beth's brothers, most of the people I consider friends are people I see one or fewer times per year.

My first big volunteer job was to assemble and distribute lawn signs promoting the organization. I had 75 signs to deliver, some to homes, and some to high-visibility intersections. In preparation for my first run, I fussed with Google Maps for a half hour trying to map out the most efficient loop to deliver to 18 houses. I thought of my college roommate, Tom Collins, who delivered pizza on the weekends in the pre-GPS days and had to make these kinds of calculations on the fly. I haven't spoken to Tom since the day after the Eagles lost the Super Bowl in February 2005, and there's a good chance we'll never see each other again. When I google him I get mostly drink recipes, but I also find someone who looks like him and is the general manager of a large bank. I wonder if he still strums his guitar at night and thinks about the days when he played in punk rock bands. I bet he's one of those parents who plays NOFX records for his kids and is weirdly proud that they like the music from his youth.

I'd volunteered to deliver the signs because it was an emergency—everything for this event was happening last-minute—and because I had the time. I was still teaching exclusively online, and sometimes went five full days in a row without ever walking out my front door. I found that I enjoyed beyond all reason the procedural detail of assembling the signs, planning an ideal route, figuring out where to leave the sign for the homeowner to find, leaving the engine running while I hopped out and drove the metal frame into the dirt—it all delivered a particular kind of satisfaction I can't really explain. LauraBeth joined me for the next few rounds—she drove while I directed her down every little side street, whole pockets of the neighborhood I'd never seen—and within a few days, we had carpeted the town in signs. I got a text from Carrie, one of the organizers, that said "I woke up today and saw four signs on the way to school! You two are amazing!" There has always been a part of me that responds especially well to being praised for following directions. It's why I was a good student. Why I would be a great juror.

Some of the signs disappeared over the next week. Weather, maybe. Unlikely in the cases where signs for other organizations were still standing but ours had been bent in half and clearly stomped on. When I saw one down, I pulled over and put it right back up. Once, while I was fighting to drive the metal prongs into drought-hardened soil, two cars drove by honking and cheering for me. I'm not sharing all this because I think I deserve applause, but because it feels good when people tell you you're good.

Like most affluent suburbs, ours is still a deeply segregated one. Despite the Blue Lives Matter and Take America Back flags spread throughout town, we reliably vote blue and poll in favor of various liberal causes. Every block is dotted with lawn signs making silly declarations like, "In this house we believe in science" or, worse, the painfully unwieldy, "Hate has no home here." (The font situation on these signs is, suffice to say, out of control.) There are little free libraries standing uselessly at every 10th house, each one full of books the homeowners feel too guilty to throw out. We check all the good liberal boxes, is my point. And yet, as of the most recent census our nice safe little town is 89.9% white, median household income is more than $30,000 higher than the U.S. average, and most people have a college degree or more. When a developer proposes the construction of affordable housing, they are met with fierce resistance about parking, about school overcrowding. All the usual complaints. On Halloween, trick-or-treat hours are limited to the absurd window of 3 to 6 PM, ostensibly to prevent mischief though it is a barely concealed secret that the real motivation is to keep kids from poorer neighborhoods from coming to town and taking "our" candy.

There are structural problems and there are individual problems, and I feel powerless most of the time. I don't think I deserve any absolution just because I'm naming the situation.

Despite lots of scrambling, the Pride weekend was a massive success. Over 7,000 people came to the parade; for many, it was the first major outdoor gathering they'd attended since the start of the pandemic. Queer and nonbinary kids ran around wrapped in pride flags and trans flags without fear of reprisal. Grown men cried in the street about how they'd been raised here and never thought it would be possible to walk down Haddon Avenue, out and proud and fearless. I can get cynical about liberal do-gooderism that feels mostly symbolic. I know that a parade and some surrounding events can only do so much to change minds, to make people safe, to combat a growing legislative assault on the lives of queer people. But to work together with a couple dozen other people and make a good day happen? To finally take a step toward integrating myself in a community? To feel useful? I don't doubt the value of any of that. You can't let yourself become too jaded to even try.

2022

The night before my 40th birthday, I had a dream about going to Dalessandro's, the famous cheesesteak shop where I worked through high school and most of college. Though I quit that job in 2003—hastily, after a fight about unfavorable schedules—I still regularly have stress dreams about it. Slips piling up, customers shouting at me, giant hunks of frozen beef that won't cook no matter how hard I hack away at them. I dream of rolls crumbling into dust in my hands. Of brown bags that never fill up no matter how many sandwiches I shove inside them. On the worst nights, I wake up coursing with adrenaline, that overwhelming sensation of being in the weeds, familiar to anyone who has worked in food service. But in this particular dream, I was a customer, and the place, which in real life hasn't been updated in any meaningful way since the early 1970s, had changed dramatically. Fresh paint and new stylish flooring and marble countertops. The fridge that used to hold 40-ounce bottles of Colt 45 was now full of craft microbrews. The grim factory vibe I knew so well had been supplanted by a joyous atmosphere. The cooks were so young they looked like a different species. Back when I was the youngest guy on the griddle, nobody knew how to talk to me. One waitress always made time to tell me that kids my age are too stupid to know anything. Another one pulled me aside one bleak Friday afternoon and warned me, "Whatever you do, do not spend the rest of your life here."

In my dream, I ordered a cheesesteak with provolone, fried onions, and pizza sauce, but they didn't have any of the ingredients I wanted. They handed me a menu, but I couldn't read it. I kept trying to tell the young guys stories about my days in their shoes and they looked through me, as if I were speaking in a frequency they couldn't hear.

I'm reluctant to attribute too much meaning to dreams, but this one seems pretty straightforward. Sometimes you do have portentous dreams and sometimes things really do symbolize other things.

The evening of my birthday, LauraBeth and I walked toward South Street in Philly for the first time since before the pandemic. With each tentative step, there was a sense of rediscovery. Restaurants we'd been to dozens of times. Bars we'd hoped to visit again but that were permanently closed. The corner on 3rd and Bainbridge where we'd once been caught in a torrential downpour while helping a friend move into his apartment. The coffee shop where I'd been served by a former student who'd gotten an F in my course and, I swear, glared at me the whole time, until I dropped a $10 bill on the table and left without taking a sip. It was all the same but it wasn't. It's hard enough to keep up with it all even in normal times.

We had dinner at a French bistro that I love, a place that had closed down for the first two years of the pandemic while the chef made ends meet by cooking private meals for clients. I ordered the exact same meal I'd had there three years earlier, probably on another birthday. Carafe of house white, oeuf du pêcheur, trout meunière. Shared crème brûlée for dessert. Inside, the only difference between then and now was that the servers wore masks. We wore masks, too, when we walked to and from the restroom, working under the theory, I suppose, that the deadly virus could only spread if we were in motion. I'm not supposed to be so flippant, but we'd all been living with it so long I didn't care anymore. I mean, I cared. But not the same way I did two years earlier. If you think about it all too much, you can fall apart.

We wanted to get a drink after dinner, and although I still think of Philly as my city, still pride myself on knowing my way around every little pocket of town, I sat there googling "bars near me" because I couldn't remember what used to be there. Couldn't even guess what was there now.

We ended up at Tattooed Mom, one of the few counterculture-type places left on South Street, which is more like a sad shopping mall these days. They checked our vaccine cards thoroughly at T-Mom's, one of the very few businesses I'd encountered that seemed to take their own precautions seriously. I led LauraBeth upstairs, where local artists have covered the walls and ceiling in so many layers of graffiti and wheatpastes and stickers and so on that the room must shrink by a few square centimeters every year. An imperceptible compression of the space until the day comes when there is no room left for anyone to stand.

Everyone else upstairs was half my age. Younger people were more likely to be out and about then anyway—most of my cohort was still taking their first tentative steps back into normalcy, many of my friends and colleagues having gone all this time without even entering a grocery store—but also everyone around me is getting younger all the time. Some days, I feel acutely that I am the only person who is aging. Other days, I feel fine. Four years ago, I was center stage in this room, reading from my critically acclaimed novel, but that was so long ago it may as well have never happened. I fooled myself for a while into thinking that moment would be transformative for my career, for my life overall. Nobody up there knew about it; there was no reason for them to. They were drunk and young and playing pool and sitting on each other's laps. Some of them were going to make catastrophic decisions that night. Some of them would think of nights like this as the best in their lives. If they noticed me, it was only because I was in their way. You don't really have a choice in whether you become obsolete or not, but I think there's some dignity in acknowledging it.

In the year leading up to your 40th birthday, there's a lot of external pressure to make a big deal about it. Even if you insist it is not a big deal. Especially if you insist. For at least six months, friends and family asked me what plans I had. Would I rent out a hall? A party boat? Some talked about their own plans, the trips, the goals to achieve beforehand—races, promotions, new hobbies. They talked about "bucket lists," and I struggled to engage because I don't even especially care for the phrase "kick the bucket," it sounds like the way a child would process death, and I admit to being an annoying pedant regarding the meaning of the term "bucket list," which I realize for most people means "some stuff I want to do someday" though it originated as literally "the final tasks I must complete before I die." I didn't want to do a big party. Eventually, a week or two later, we did a medium party, and everyone had a nice time. My youngest niece gave me a hand-made card with a drawing of a rainbow and the message: *Uncle Tom—You are SO OLD.*

That night at dinner, before we went out to the bar and surrounded ourselves with young people, the waitress asked if we were celebrating anything. When I said it was my 40th birthday, she rubbed my shoulder, leaned in, and asked me, sincerely, if my day had been okay. If I felt okay. I said I did. I said it really just felt like another day. She said, "When I turned 30, I sat under my covers alone all day and cried. But when I turned 40, I woke up and didn't feel anything at all. I got out of bed and I said, *Fuck it, that's all there is.*"

2023

A few days ago, I rode my bike 1.1 miles from my house to my third favorite coffee shop, the one that sells R&B records as well as bootleg DVDs of 1990s action films. I went there because it is the safest one to get to by bike and because according to LauraBeth, they have the best iced tea in town. We rode together, me in the lead, and then we sat outside on their makeshift patio. The barista here always makes eye contact for longer than you expect, and asks, "Have you done anything interesting today?" I've avoided going there sometimes because I don't have a good answer to the question. Often, the only thing I've done on a given day is I have gone to that coffee shop.

The weather was suited perfectly to bike riding, the kind of afternoon you get maybe 10 times a year and for which you move to a so-called "15-minute suburb" in the first place. The whole point of living in a place like this is so that you can ride your bike aimlessly on a nice day. It was the 10th time in my life I had ever ridden a bike. Nine of them have occurred within the past year.

Last summer, I found a free course in Philly for adults who wanted to learn how to ride bikes. The incident that finally pushed me over the edge was when my eight-year-old niece was riding in circles around me, baffled by my inability to do the same. She asked why I'm afraid to do something so easy. I was afraid—of falling, sure, but mostly of looking foolish. Of struggling to even get on the seat at a public park and then throwing a tantrum while some teens recorded me on their phones. I was afraid of finding out how limited I really am. I liked the idea of taking a class, of not being the only one. Having a teacher who I could listen to and try to please.

We met under the I-95 overpass in South Philly—four students and three instructors. I got there a half hour early, so I sat in my car waiting for someone else to arrive. I saw a man in his early fifties get dropped off by a person I later learned was his daughter. He paced around at the meeting spot for a few minutes, then stood on the corner smoking a cigarette, then paced around again, and then I joined him. His name was Neil, and he had been raised in Peru. He asked if I was nervous, and I said I wasn't; this was mostly true. I was eager to finally move on with my life. "This is a good thing we are doing," he said. "It's one of the best things."

The rest of the group arrived shortly thereafter. The instructors asked us to introduce ourselves and share our motivation for taking the class. One woman had been an active cyclist through her early twenties, but hadn't gotten back on a bike since a bad fall many years ago. Another was a college student who had never in her life been on a bike. She was going to spend the next year living with family in Vietnam, and they'd told her she needed to be prepared to ride long distances with them. I said I was there because I was tired of letting my wife down, thinking of the many times on vacation when we could have rented bikes and explored some new area together, if not for my inadequacies. Neil said, "I have always wanted to do this, but I've been too afraid."

I hadn't told anyone besides LauraBeth about this class; I didn't want to have to explain myself if I failed. I reassured myself I was a physically capable adult, that I was only trying to learn a skill that five-year-olds around the world master every day. We spent the first 20 minutes standing in one spot, kickstand in place. We practiced mounting the bike and sitting still. We moved one pedal, then the other. We released and re-engaged the kickstand. Neil struggled to move the kickstand with his foot, and there was a five-minute delay while we watched him grow increasingly flustered as he tried to figure it out. The class was scheduled for two hours, and I began to think we might need to come back for a second session. Then the instructor told us to strap on our helmets and glide down the (slight) hill without pedaling. We walked our bikes back up the hill and glided down again. After a few repetitions, we then glided down the hill with our feet on the pedals. It wasn't until we began to incorporate pedaling that it became difficult. It required all my concentration to guide the bike in something resembling a straight line. Turning around while in motion seemed like a task better suited for two strapping men and a team of oxen. Still, for brief flashes, I was cruising. At the bottom of the hill, after another failed turn, I stood next to Neil, both of us glazed in sweat. He said, "Tom, I can't do this." I had no advice. He said, "Why is it so easy for the rest of you?" He could barely keep his feet on the pedals when the bike was stationary. After two more failed rotations, he walked his bike back to the rack, whispered something to the instructor, and then trudged away, phone pressed to his ear. I imagine he was calling his daughter, telling her he'd failed, and it had been a mistake to try. By the end of hour two, I managed to go up and down the hill four consecutive times without stopping; the instructors cheered as they recorded a video of me, on wheels and in motion and under control.

Afterward, I drove further into South Philly to reward myself with a roast pork sandwich, and while I ate, I texted the video to LauraBeth first, then to my mom and Kevin, who were happy for me but mainly shocked, as if I'd texted them that I'd decided to grow five inches overnight. I posted it to a couple group chats, and as much as I tried to downplay it there, I was inordinately proud. To think that, even as you get older, you can still learn. You can still improve your life, you don't have to cheat yourself out of exploring new pathways. It's easy, sometimes, to mistake a lack of skill as an affliction you're born with; in some ways my life has been defined by the paths I haven't taken, out of fear or spite or pettiness. I've watched older people in my family gradually succumb to the narrowing of their worlds. Sometimes, it's not within their control—they get sick or injured and they cannot physically live as they once did. Often, it's been more insidious, a long series of compromises, of sacrificing opportunities, of allowing friendships and outside interests and ambitions to erode until they grew barely recognizable. My father-in-law was like this in his final years—where once he had been a gregarious and playful man, he now spent his days sitting in the dark, watching TV and feeling badly all the time. As the quality of his life steadily degraded, you could see that some part of him was convinced it was his fault, that he had never deserved anything better. I'm not arrogant enough to think I can fully prevent this kind of decline—the indignities we face are relentless, and it doesn't take much to break someone down. But I think about riding a bike and I remember: it's still possible to grow and change.

I've been checking the cycling instructor's Twitter feed, hoping to see a video of Neil, having returned to class and tried again. Hoping to see his expression the moment it all clicks into place and he feels himself, riding and free. So far, he has not turned up.

I'm still building confidence on the bike, but am now competent enough to ride alone, in traffic and around potholes and past barking dogs and over curbs. I can roll out of my garage right now and cruise through my neighborhood, seeing it from an entirely new perspective. I try to imagine what I look like to my neighbors through their windows. I cannot help but indulge the fantasy of being a character in a television show, someone they don't just glance at but think about in their free time. I wonder whether they can see the version of me that I want them to see: a version of me that is kinder, bolder, smarter. More confident and more artful and more loving and more reliable. A man who is open to all the universe has to offer him.

2024

After several years of steadily intensifying pain, my mom had her right knee replaced in January. She worked 49 years as a nurse and in her retirement has endured an endless string of orthopedic procedures—wrist, spine, foot, wrist again, knee, and so on—and although she is dogged in maintaining her physical therapy regimen, some days her morale dips as low as it's ever been. When we talk on the phone, sometimes she sounds exhausted, having spent all day calling insurance companies or lying still for an MRI or waiting in lines at pharmacies. She and her husband live in an over-55 community, so they're surrounded by people their age and older, each with their own complicated medical histories, many in various stages of physical and mental decline. She did not want to get this surgery; she'd heard from friends that the recovery was too painful, and she'd been saying for months that her knee pain was at only an eight or nine on a 10-point scale. "I can deal with an eight or nine," she'd say. I would ask if she wouldn't rather it be less than that; maybe the pain had been there so long she'd forgotten what it was like to live without it?

I think on some level she knew her resistance was not entirely rational; simultaneous to our conversations, she was convincing her closest friend it was time to have her hip replaced. When we visited my mom two days after she finally had her own knee surgery, she was on the phone with this friend, saying, "It's not as bad as you think," and after she hung up she told us, "The pain is so much worse than I thought."

She only lives about 35 minutes away, so we've been visiting her every weekend while she's recovering, and the last time I saw

159

her she was already moving freely about the house, carrying but not really using a cane. She told us how difficult physical therapy had been the previous day, and LauraBeth tried to remind her that it's a triumph, one month after surgery, to be riding a recumbent bicycle, stepping over a series of cones, rising out of a chair without using her arms. My mom knows these are all victories but discusses them in a tone that suggests they're failures; I know this mindset intimately.

On that visit, we had cake and tea and sat at her dining room table, where 10 prescription pill bottles were arranged as a pharmaceutical centerpiece. She told us about everyone in her church who had recently had body parts surgically replaced, and I realized that, if we're lucky, we will live to an age where this is the main mode of conversation: what's been going wrong with me lately. Part of me looks forward to it, to having new problems to complain about, to having friends and acquaintances who genuinely want to know all about my bad ankle and my arthritis and whatever falls apart next.

A couple months before this surgery, we took a short trip to Orlando with my mom and her husband. My mom had been talking for years about going to the Disney Food & Wine Festival. While I griped about the obscene cost of all things Disney, LauraBeth reminded me again that we need to enjoy these opportunities with her while we can. I don't have much to tell you about Disney World, besides that a shocking number of the people we saw at EPCOT were as drunk as college football fans at a tailgate. We went on some rides and tried some foods from the international stands and bustled through sweaty crowds and stood in lines sometimes as long as two hours. At night we drank wine in the hotel and talked about the same topics we always talk about.

My mom's friend Anne lives two hours from Orlando and she's dying. They met in nursing school and have been close ever since, even with Anne moving around the southeast U.S. for the past four decades. We visited Anne and her family a few times when I was growing up. I vividly remember being 11 and sitting with her son beside a basketball court—we'd brought a ball but some teenagers had taken over the court—and swapping stories we'd heard about older kids in our schools doing drugs and having sex. "Yeah," he said, solemnly, "Sex. There's a lot of that around here too." I nodded, agreeing that probably sex was everywhere at that point. We were on the verge of a breakthrough.

Anne has a brain tumor and has suffered a few strokes, and her husband's life is now devoted to her care, to trying to milk whatever pleasure they can out of the time she has left. On our Disney trip, we drove down to Anne's house so my mom could visit her, almost certainly for the last time in person. After dropping her off, we went out for coffee nearby with my mom's husband. Sitting outside the coffee shop, LauraBeth saw a shrub in the parking lot smoldering. I watched the smoke rising and then I watched the shrub combust, and then I wondered whether I was supposed to do anything about it. An armed guard from a nearby store ran outside and stomped on the fire, and then spent the next 10 minutes running between a pizza place and the shrub with buckets of ice. By the time we left, the fire had been extinguished and I'd had nothing to do with any of it, but I was glad to have a new story to tell.

My mom had been worried that Anne would be too addled from her strokes and her medications to recognize her, but she said that Anne was relatively lucid. They reminisced for a half hour and then hugged and posed for a nice photo, which is now printed and taped on the glass window of the china cabinet beside my mom's dining room table. After my mom's surgery, sipping on tea, we rehashed all of this: the drunks at EPCOT, the burning bush, the photo with Anne. Kevin had joined us on this visit too, and I was glad for it; he is better than me at letting people talk, about indulging them when they're telling stories we've all heard several times already.

We often repeat stories, and repeat them again, during these visits. Sometimes they take an unexpected turn or include a new detail—a cousin my mom has never mentioned before, a family fight never revealed. These aren't exactly secrets being exposed, just old stories never told. I assume in some cases my mom has forgotten them entirely until they come up. In others, she made a choice not to tell us until we were older. The specifics of these conversations aren't the point, not here; the point is their existence at all, knowing that there are parts of my family and history I can never fully understand, not with the time we have in front of us. The point is that as I get older I'm greedy for these stories and I also need to make my peace with never hearing them all.

When I say Kevin is better than me at this kind of conversation, what I mean is I think Kevin is happier than I am. I think a lot of people are. When I say happy, I mean content. I tell myself often that I am content, but when I say that what I mean is something more like secure. When I say Kevin is happier than I am, that a lot of people are, what I mean is it seems like most people in my life have a greater capacity for joy than I do. I mean that when it's time to see friends and family, he probably puts on his jacket and goes, whereas it takes me hours of self-talk to get over my natural inclination to never leave the house.

As we've been getting older and friends' parents are dying, friends' spouses are dying, friends are enduring any number of crises, LauraBeth keeps telling me: the most important thing you can do is show up. I'm trying, more than I used to, to show up. To make plans and follow through on them. The truth is, I almost always enjoy myself when I do, but somehow I forget in the interim. When I say enjoy myself, I mean I feel more like a person who is alive. When I say alive, what I mean is I can sense and see my own body, can understand my thoughts, can understand myself as significant to other people who are also alive, like me, and trying to make it all work.

ACKNOWLEDGMENTS

Many chapters of this book have previously appeared (in somewhat different forms) in all manner of literary journals. I'm grateful to the editors for their support and their careful attention to my work. I've listed them below in mostly chronological order:

"1983" & "1997" *Call Me* [*Brackets*]
"1984" & "2019" *Pithead Chapel*
"1988" *Juked*
"1991" & "2003" *Sundog Lit*
"1992" *What Are Birds*
"1993," "2017," & "2022" *Epoch*
"1994" *Hobart*
"1995" *Waxwing*
"1996" *The Citron Review*
"1998" *The Rupture*
"2001" & "2004" *Laurel Review*
"2002" *Schuylkill Valley Review*
"2003" *Sundog Lit*
"2005" *X-Ray*
"2006" *Superstition Review*
"2007" *Pine Hills Review*
"2008" *Gigantic Sequins*
"2010" *Jellyfish Review*
"2011" *The Fourth River*
"2012" *Swamp Ape Review*
"2013" *Atticus Review*

"2016" *Cherry Tree*
"2018" *Peach Mag*

I am forever grateful to LauraBeth for tolerating this weird hobby of mine, and also for being the greatest friend and partner of my life.

I am thankful also to my family, who don't need me to name them because they know who they are and why they're here.

My home base in the literary world has always been the *Barrelhouse* team; without them, I probably would have quit a long time ago. Thanks for letting me keep on hanging around.

To everyone at ST, thanks for keeping it w4w.

As of the time I am writing this note, I have left my job at Temple University for a new position at Rutgers-Camden. Thank you to everyone at Temple who supported me—as a teacher and a writer—and tolerated my many failures as I was learning how to do the job. And thanks in advance to the Rutgers staff and students for the same.

ABOUT THE AUTHOR

Tom McAllister is the author of the novel *How to Be Safe*, which was named one of the best books of 2018 by *Kirkus* and *The Washington Post*. His other books are the novel *The Young Widower's Handbook* and the memoir *Bury Me in My Jersey*. His short stories and essays have been published in *The Sun*, *Best American Nonrequired Reading*, *Black Warrior Review*, and many other places. He is the nonfiction editor at *Barrelhouse* and co-hosts the *Book Fight!* podcast with Mike Ingram. He lives in New Jersey and teaches in the MFA Program at Rutgers-Camden. Visit his website at tom.mcallister.ws.

A NOTE ABOUT THE TYPE

On the cover, the book title is set in Orpheus Pro, a revival serif that was released by Canada Type in 2011. It combines two original font designs by Walter Tiemann: Orpheus, which was released in the late 1920s, and Euphorion, an italic companion to Orpheus that debuted in 1936. The letterforms have calligraphic features and a sharp elegance that suits the keen observations of the essays in *It All Felt Impossible*.

The body of the book is set in Freight Text, a practical serif inspired by 18th-century Dutch fonts. It was designed by Joshua Darden and released in 2005 through GarageFonts, a type foundry based in Pennsylvania, the same state where author Tom McAllister grew up. On the *Talk Paper Scissors* podcast, host Diana Varma describes Freight as "unique enough to catch the eyes but comfortable enough to keep them from bleeding."

The interior display font is set in IBM Plex Mono, a monospaced type that's part of the IBM Plex family. It was released in 2017 and combines characteristics of computerized modernity with old-fashioned typewriter styles to create a harmonious blend of past and present, much as the author does with this book. The font is reminiscent of those used in the video games and computer programs from the 1980s and 90s mentioned in the essays on the first decades of McAllister's life.

—Heather Butterfield